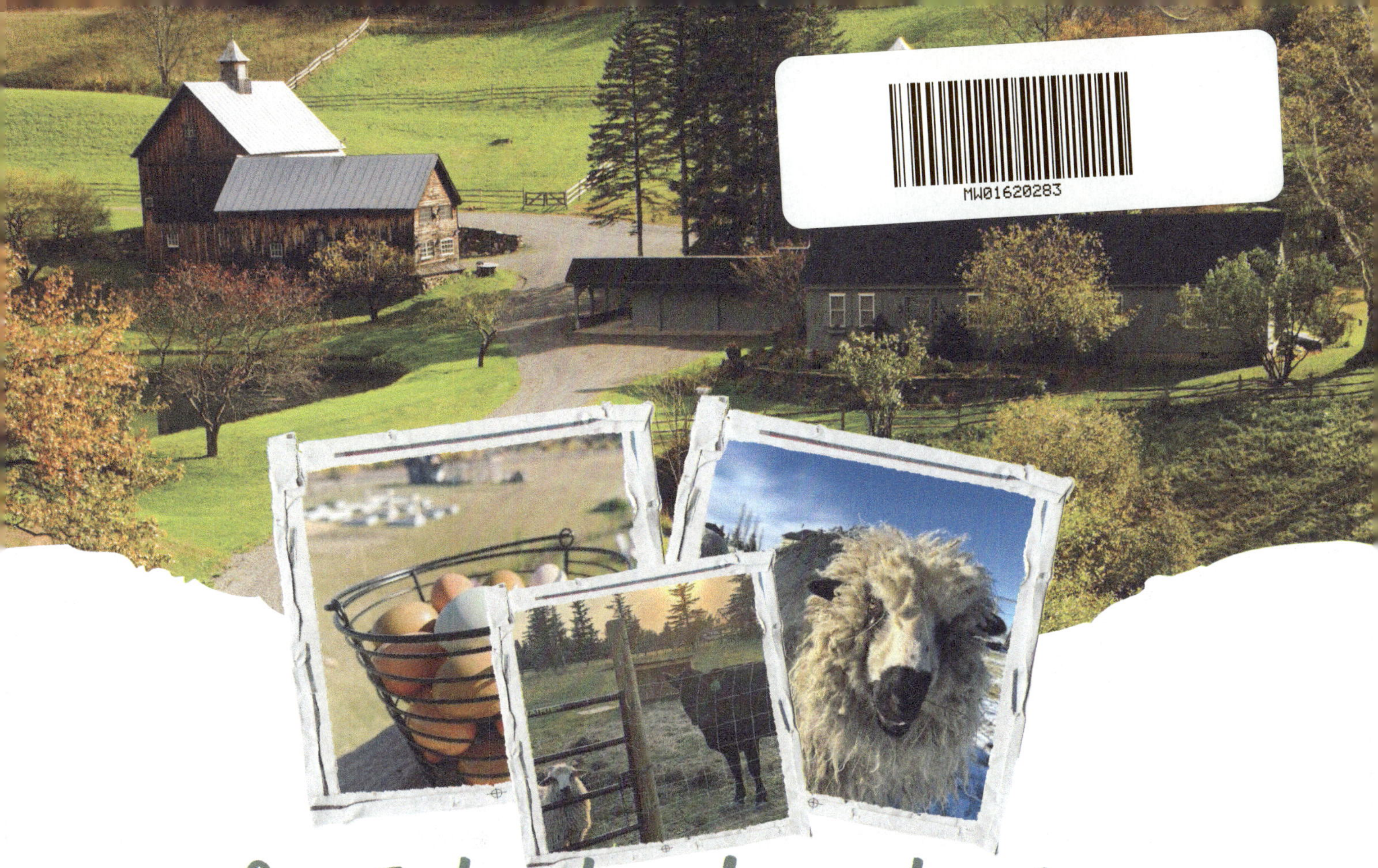

An Intro to Homesteading:

A CHILDREN'S WORKBOOK FOR HOMESCHOOLERS

Deer Creek Homestead Welcomes You!

Welcome to An Intro to Homesteading: A workbook for Homeschoolers curriculum! Back in 2022 we decided to leave the big city behind and start a homestead! We have been enjoying this peaceful life, seeking to be more self-sustainable, and are excited to share what we have learned with you!

This mini-course will introduce you to the basics of homesteading, including raising livestock, making your own food, growing your own food, and creating/making your own household items (mixing, crafting, forming, etc.). I hope you enjoy learning these new skills as much as we do!

Daniel & Amanda Preston

WWW.THEDEERCREEKHOMESTEAD.COM

Book Cover by Amanda Preston
Illustrations by Canva
First edition 2025

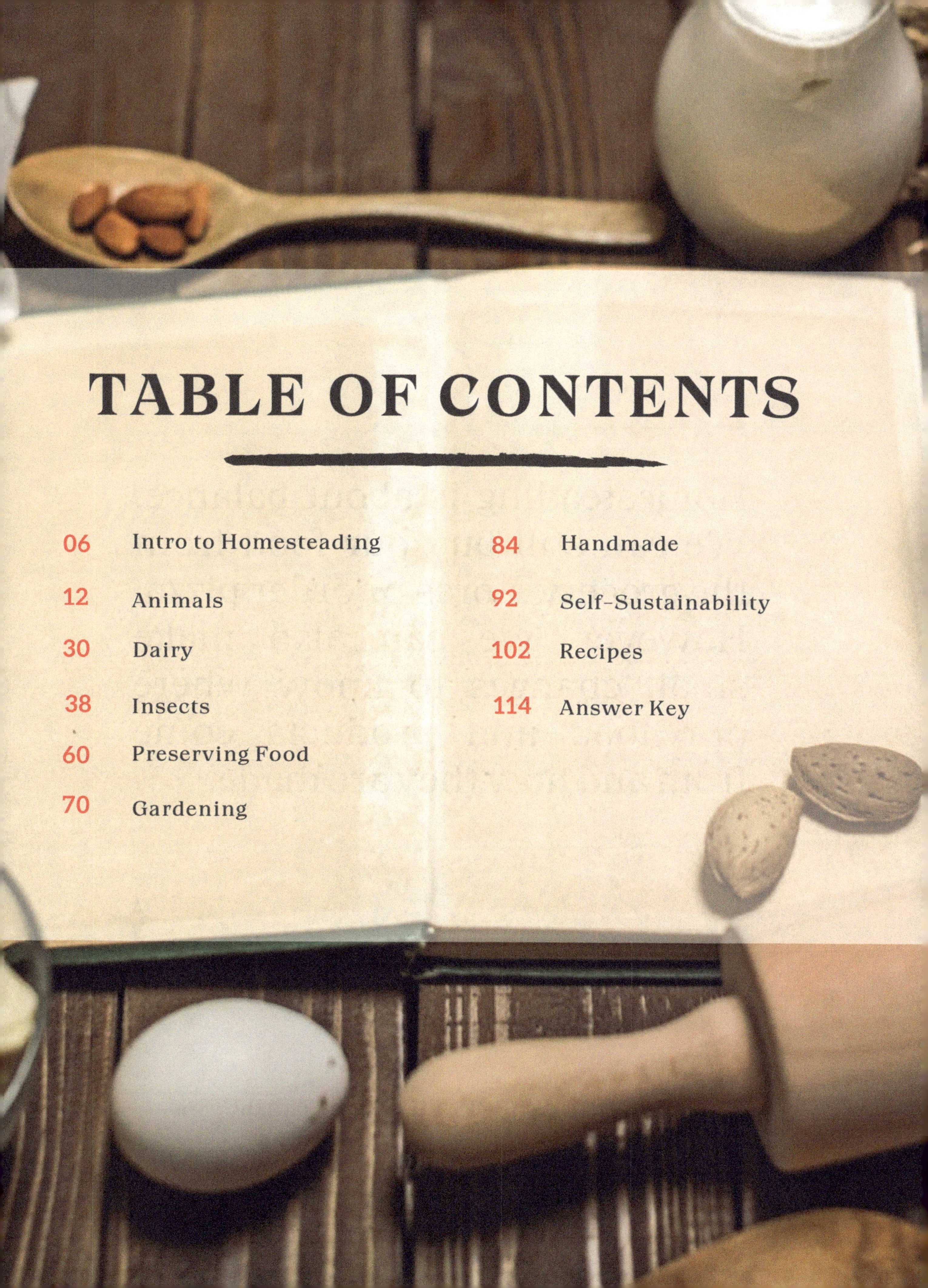

TABLE OF CONTENTS

Homesteading is about balance. We can still buy our food from the grocery stores or order pizza. However, we can also make small changes to know where our food and products come from and how they are made.

HOMESTEADING

AN INTRODUCTION

WHAT IS A HOMESTEADING?

Homesteading is a lifestyle of self-sustainability, often centered around a family home and farm. It can involve growing food, preserving food, raising animals, and making crafts.

OTHER TERMS

Homesteading may also be referred to as farmsteading, hobby farming, off-grid living and farming.

MODERN HOMESTEADING

Modern homesteaders often use renewable energy options including solar and wind power. Many also choose to plant and grow heirloom vegetable and to raise heritage livestock. Homesteading is not defined by where someone lives, such as the city or the country, but by the lifestyle choices they make.

BACKGROUND

Homesteading is a lifestyle of self sustainability. It is characterized by subsistence agriculture, home preservation of food, and may also involve the small scale production of textiles, clothing, and craft work for household use or sale. Homesteading has been pursued in various ways around the world and throughout different historical eras. It is typically distinguished from rural village or commune living by the isolation of the homestead (socially, physically, or both).

The History of Homesteading

Homesteading in Canada & US

United States 1862

Use of the term "homesteading" began in 1862 when the U.S. gave 160 acres to each U.S. Citizen who would live on it for at least 5 years.

Indigenous People

The government homestead expansion endeavor resulted in the violent relocation of many Indigenous people.

Global

Homesteading has been practiced throughout history around the world. In the UK they say "smallholder" or "croft."

Renewed in the 1930/1940's.

Renewed interest in homesteading was brought about by U.S. President Franklin Roosevelt's program of Subsistence Homesteading in the 1930s and 1940s.

Expansion

Historically, homesteading has been used by governmental entities with national expansion to help settle what were termed unsettled areas, especially in the United States, Canada, and Australia.

Current Homesteading

Homesteaders now often include families brand new to the homestead life with little to no experience.

Name: ______________________ Date: ______________________

Homesteading Basics

Fill in the blanks below about the basics of homesteading using the words provided:

animals	experience	1862	lives	growing	farmsteading	preserving
wind	expansion	heirloom	crafts	relocation	self-sustainability	

1. Homesteading is a lifestyle of ______________ .
2. Homesteading can include ______________ and ______________ food.
3. Homesteading can involve raising ______________ .
4. Homesteading can use solar and ______________ power.
5. The term homesteading first began in the US in ______________ .
6. Homesteading requires little to no ______________ .
7. Homesteading was used by the government for national ______________ .
8. Homesteading is not defined by where someone ______________ .
9. Homesteaders enjoying making ______________ .
10. Homesteaders grow ______________ vegetables and heritage livestock.
11. Homesteading is also known as ______________ .
12. Homesteading expansion resulted in the violent ______________ of many Indigenous people.

Name: ____________________ Date: ____________________

Flower Coloring

Color & create the most amazing flower

DEER CREEK

HOMESTEAD

COMMON PRACTICES

RAISING CHICKENS

GROWING GARDENS

MAKING HOMEMADE FOOD

KEEPING BEES

STARTING A FARM

COLLECTING RAINWATER

FOOD PRESERVATION

WOODWORKING & CRAFTWORK

Making Your Own Food

List store bought foods you could make at home:

PANTRY FOODS

REFRIGERATOR FOODS

HOUSEHOLD ITEMS

ANIMALS

Draw your favorite farm animal:

DEER CREEK

HOMESTEAD

COMMON USES FOR ANIMALS

EATING THEIR MEAT

USING THEIR WOOL

DRINKING THEIR MILK

USING THEIR EGGS

USING THEIR FAT (TALLOW, LANOLIN)

USING THEIR FEATHERS (FISHING LURES)

CARE FOR THE LAND

PROTECT OTHER ANIMALS (LLAMA)

Using Your Animals

List products you can make from animals:

FOOD PRODUCTS

PERSONAL CARE

HOUSEHOLD ITEMS

CHICKEN FACTS

MALE AND FEMALE BABIES ARE CALLED CHICKS

FEMALE CHICKEN UNDER 1 YEARS OLD IS CALLED A PULLET

MALE CHICKEN UNDER 1 YEARS OLD IS CALLED A COCKEREL

FEMALE ADULT IS CALLED A HEN. THE MALE IS CALLED A ROOSTER.

CHICKENS CAN RECOGNIZE UP TO 100 FACES

CHICKENS LIVE FOR 5-10 YEARS

CHICKENS ARE OMNIVORES AND EAT FRUITS, VEGGIES, GRAINS, AND MICE!

ANATOMY OF A CHICKEN

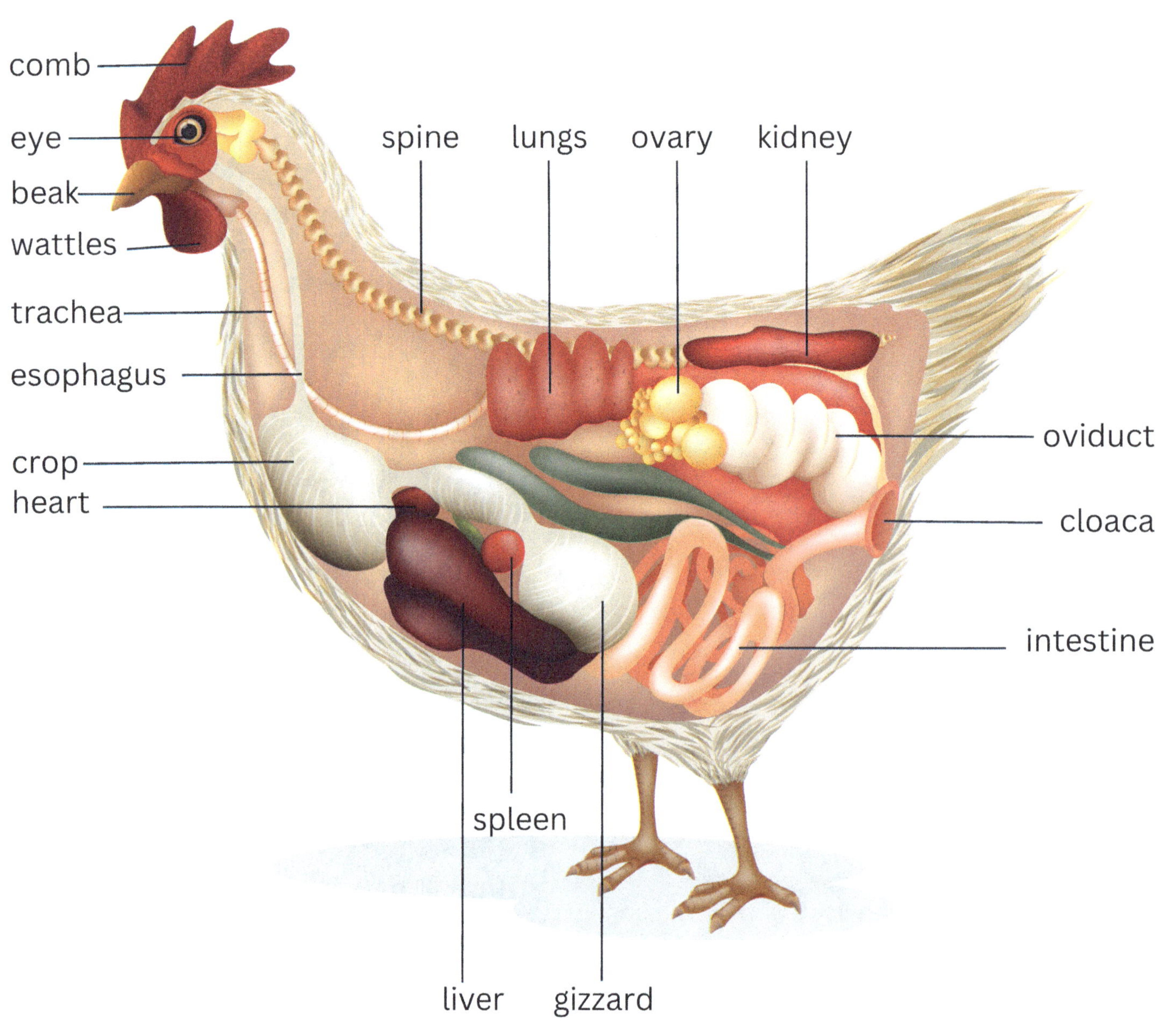

COW FACTS

CALF IS A BABY COW

HEIFER IS A YOUNG FEMALE THAT HAS NOT HAD A CALF

STEER IS A CASTRATED MALE

COW IS A MATURE FEMALE THAT HAS HAD AT LEAST 1 CALF

BULL IS A MATURE INTACT MALE THAT IS USED FOR BREEDING

COWS USUALLY LIVE FOR 15-20 YEARS

MOST COWS ARE SLAUGHTERED AT 18 MONTHS OLD

ANATOMY OF A COW

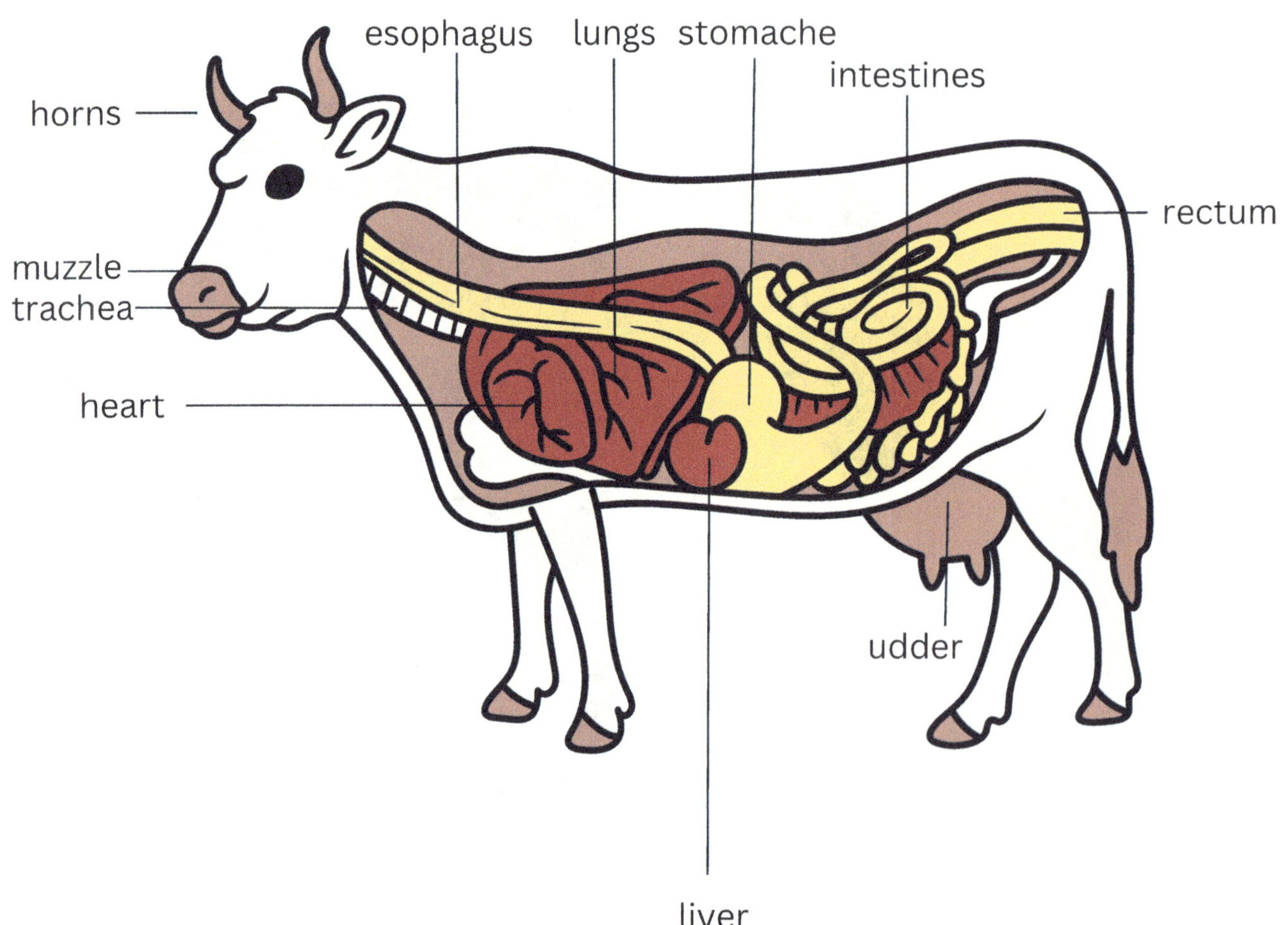

CUTS OF BEEF

Provide examples of types of beef you might buy:

____________________ ____________________

____________________ ____________________

____________________ ____________________

____________________ ____________________

Name: Date:

COWS

WORD SEARCH

Can you find all the cow related words?

C	L	E	F	O	R	A	S	I	Z	Z	A
B	A	K	R	C	A	L	F	N	Y	A	I
S	Q	L	E	R	A	I	E	T	O	R	P
T	W	I	F	R	P	G	N	M	R	A	E
E	H	M	G	S	L	A	R	F	O	O	H
E	E	F	E	I	L	D	E	A	T	R	R
R	A	T	S	N	R	O	H	F	S	W	Y
R	T	O	A	E	T	C	C	G	I	S	U
T	O	T	F	O	G	B	U	L	L	U	D
U	T	I	E	U	O	C	E	G	M	L	D
N	E	I	N	P	E	O	R	A	N	E	E
H	H	N	A	R	B	W	B	E	E	F	R

COW	CALF	HOOF	HORNS
HEIFER	MILK	STEER	UDDER
BULL	GRASS	BEEF	FEILD

SHEEP FACTS

A BABY SHEEP IS CALLED A LAMB

A FEMALE IS CALLED A EWE AND A MALE IS CALLED A RAM

A MALE THAT CAN'T HAVE BABIES IS CALLED A WETHER

SHEEP LIVE FOR 10-12 YEARS

SHEEP CAN RECOGNIZE UP TO 50 SHEEP FACES

SHEEPS HAVE A GREAT SENSE OF SMALL

SHEEP ARE EXCELLENT AT DISTINGUISHING BETWEEN HUMAN FACES

Name : ....

Date : ....

FILL THE MISSING LETTER

Directions: Fill in the blanks with missing letters.

C O ....

.... E .... F E R

W .... T .... E ....

P .... L L .... T

U .... D .... R

SHEEP

SHEEP ARE EXCELLENT ANIMALS TO HAVE ON A HOMESTEAD. THEY PROVIDE MILK, WOOL, MEAT, AND COMPANIONSHIP!

Sheep are excellent animals to have on a homestead and are incredibly friendly as outdoor pets as well! They don't require a ton of land, are easy to care for, and can help mow your lawn too!

MILK: Sheep milk is a nutritious alternative to cow's milk, boasting higher levels of fat solids, protein, and minerals, and is often considered easier to digest. It's also a natural source of A2 protein and contains beneficial fats, vitamins, and minerals.

WOOL: Raw wool can be used for compost, mulch, nesting, fertilizer, and cleaning. Processed wool can be used for bedding, stuffing, insulation, lanolin, yarn, textiles, crafting, and clothes.

MEAT: When sheep meat is consumed when the sheep is under 1 years old, it is called lamb. When the sheep is over a year old, it is called mutton and has a more gamey flavor.

ANATOMY OF A CHICKEN

COMPLETE THE CHICKEN ANATOMY FOR EACH PART:

ANATOMY OF A COW

Complete the cow anatomy for each part:

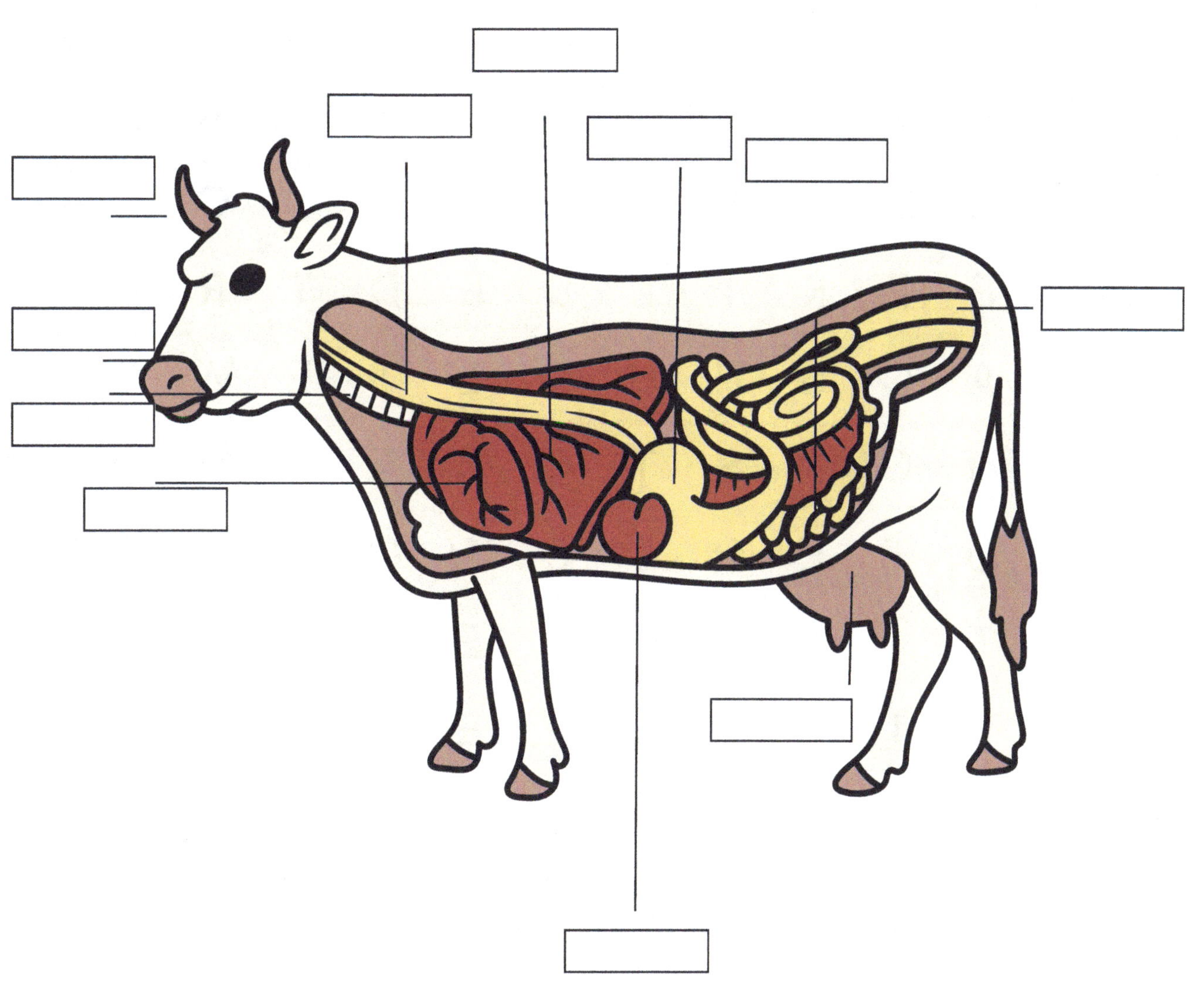

Name: Date:

FARM ANIMALS

WORD SEARCH

Can you find all the farm animal related words?

C	L	E	F	O	R	A	L	I	A	U	Q
B	Y	E	K	N	O	D	F	N	Y	U	T
R	Q	L	E	R	A	I	E	T	A	R	N
A	W	I	C	H	I	C	K	E	N	A	A
B	H	M	G	L	L	A	M	A	O	O	S
B	E	F	K	I	L	D	E	D	T	R	A
I	A	C	S	N	B	O	L	T	E	W	E
T	U	O	P	S	T	C	C	A	I	H	H
D	O	T	E	O	C	O	W	O	G	I	P
U	T	I	E	U	O	C	E	G	M	L	D
N	E	I	H	P	E	P	R	A	N	E	E
H	O	R	S	E	B	L	B	M	U	F	R

SHEEP CHICKEN RABBIT COW

PIG GOAT QUAIL PHEASANT

LLAMA DONKEY DUCK HORSE

Name: Date:

Animals Quiz

How much do you know about farm animals?
Read and choose the correct options and find out!

1 A baby sheep is called a:

a) Calf
b) Ewe
c) Lamb

2 How long do chickens live for?

a) 10-15 years
b) 1-2 years
c) 5-7 years

3 What is a male cow called?

a) Steer
b) Bull
c) Ram

4 What does not come from a sheep?

a) Milk
b) Wool
c) Eggs

5 What animal does not provide milk?

a) Goat
b) Chicken
c) Cow

6 A baby chicken is called a:

a) Hen
b) Pullet
c) Chick

7 What animal is not normally found on a homestead?

a) Tiger
b) Chicken
c) Cow

8 What animal can protect other animals on a homestead?

a) Llama
b) Chicken
c) Sheep

9 What item does not come from animals?

a) Eggs
b) Meat
c) Vegetables

10 The udder produces what?

a) Eggs
b) Milk
c) Water

Name: Date:

Color by Number

Use the color key below.

DAIRY

Draw your favorite food made with milk:

LET'S COMPARE PASTEURIZED MILK & RAW MILK

PASTEURIZED MILK	RAW MILK
 HAS BEEN HEATED TO KILL HARMFUL BACTERIA	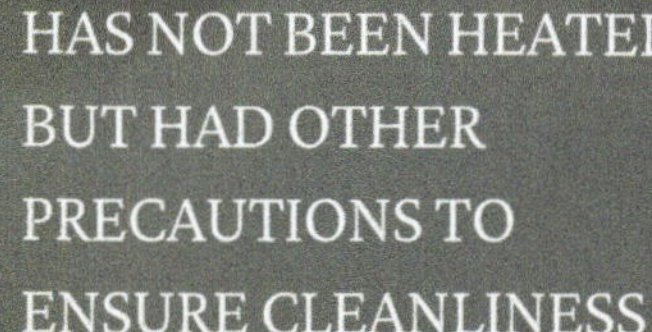 HAS NOT BEEN HEATED BUT HAD OTHER PRECAUTIONS TO ENSURE CLEANLINESS
 CAN BE PURCHASED FROM THE GROCERY STORE	 USUALLY MUST BE SOURCED FROM A FARM OR CERTIFIED PROVIDER
 MANY OF THE HELPFUL NUTRIENTS AND BACTERIA GET KILLED OFF DURING PASTEURIZATION	 HAS IMMUNE BUILDING PROPERTIES AND MICROBIOME FRIENDLY TRAITS
 CAN BE DIFFICULT TO DIGEST, WITH MANY DAIRY ALLERGIES	 MANY PEOPLE ALLERGIC TO DAIRY ARE ABLE TO CONSUME RAW MILK

*RAW MILK HAS BEEN USED FOR THE LAST 10,000 YEARS!

Dairy Products

List animals you can get milk products from:

List items you can make with milk:

BUTTER CHURNING

HOMEMADE BUTTER OFFERS SEVERAL BENEFITS, INCLUDING: CONTROL OVER INGREDIENTS, FRESHNESS, AND NUTRIENT RICHNESS, POTENTIALLY BOOSTING IMMUNITY, BONE HEALTH, AND OVERALL WELL-BEING, WHILE AVOIDING ADDITIVES AND PRESERVATIVES FOUND IN STORE-BOUGHT ALTERNATIVES.

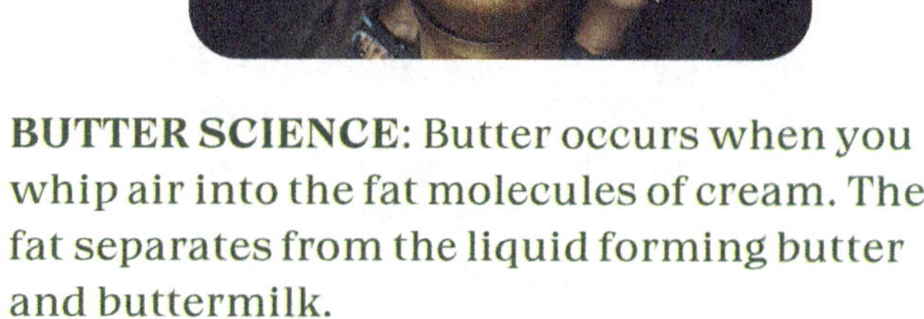

BUTTER SCIENCE: Butter occurs when you whip air into the fat molecules of cream. The fat separates from the liquid forming butter and buttermilk.

PROCESS: To make butter, leave heavy whipping cream out for 30 minutes. Pour into your stand mixer and mix on medium high. Once it looks like whipping cream, keep going! You will begin to see liquid forming. Keep going! You want most of the butter to be inside the whisk and buttermilk remaining in the bowl.

RINSE THE BUTTER: Once the butter is formed, mold it into a ball and put into a bowl of chilled or ice water and squeeze to rinse the butter. The water should look cloudy. Pour out the water and buttermilk residue, and repeat this process 3 times until the water runs clear.

STORAGE: If all the buttermilk has been rinsed out, it should last in the fridge for 2-3 weeks, less time if any buttermilk remains. Do not leave homemade butter on the counter.

Try to find butter from grass-fed cows for ultimate nutrients and health benefits!

CHEESE MAKING

AN INTRODUCTION

WHAT IS A CHEESEMAKING?

Cheesemaking, also known as caseiculture, is the process of transforming milk into cheese, a food that allows for the preservation of milk's nutritional value in a concentrated form, resulting in a wide variety of flavors and textures.

ON THE HOMESTEAD

Cheesemaking is a great way to preserve excess milk on the homestead. It also reduces the amount of chemicals.

Cheesemaking is a form of fermentation where the bacterial cultures ferment milk's lactose to produce lactic acid.

BASIC STEPS IN CHEESEMAKING

Acidification: The process of adding acid to the milk, often through the addition of cultures, which lowers the pH and helps the milk to coagulate.

Coagulation: This is the key step where milk proteins (casein) are made to clump together, forming a solid mass (curd) and separating from the liquid whey.

Rennet: A common method of coagulation involves the addition of rennet, an enzyme that helps to coagulate the milk.

Cutting the Curd: The solid curd is cut into small pieces, allowing the whey to be released, which affects the final texture of the cheese.

Cooking the Curd (Optional): For some cheese types, the curds are cooked to further expel whey and change the texture.

Salting: Salt is added to the cheese to enhance flavor, control moisture, and inhibit microbial growth.

Shaping: The curds are formed into the desired shape and size for the cheese.

Ripening and Aging: The cheese is aged under specific conditions (temperature, humidity, etc.) to develop its characteristic flavors and textures.

Cheesemaking

List as many types of cheese as you can:

Name: ______________________ Date: ______________________

All About Dairy

Fill in the blanks below about dairy products using the words provided:

immune	**raw milk**	**curds**	**butter**	**preserve**	**pasteurized**	
rinse	**buttermilk**	**goats**	**cultures**	**yogurt**	**cheddar**	**fermentation**

1. Milk that has been heated is called ____________ milk.
2. When you mix heavy cream it makes ____________ and ____________ .
3. Milk that comes straight from the cow is called ____________ .
4. Raw milk has ____________ building properties.
5. Milk can come from sheep, cows, yaks, and ____________ .
6. ____________ is a popular type of cheese.
7. The solid that forms when making cheese is called ____________ .
8. Making cheese is a great way to ____________ extra milk. .
9. Cheesemaking is a form of ____________ .
10. Make sure to ____________ the butter to avoid it going rancid.
11. Milk can be used to make ____________ , ice cream, cheese, and butter.
12. Milk requires the addition of acid or bacteria ____________ to make the milk coagulate.

INSECTS

Draw your favorite insect:

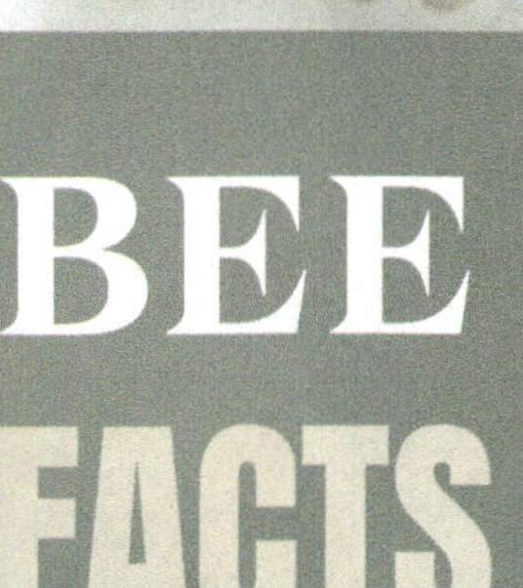

BEE FACTS

A QUEEN BEE LIVES 3-5 YEARS

WORKER BEES LIVE 2-6 WEEKS, SOMETIMES LONGER IN THE WINTER.

QUEEN BEES LAY UP TO 1,500 EGGS PER DAY

ONE BEE WILL ONLY MAKE 1/2 TSP OF HONEY IT'S ENTIRE LIFE

NECTAR IS HIGH IN NATURAL SUGAR WHICH GIVES BEES ENERGY

BEES NEVER SLEEP

EACH HIVE CONTAINS 1 QUEEN BEE, WORKER BEES (FEMALE) AND DRONE BEES (MALE)

BEEKEEPING

MANY HOMESTEADS PRACTICE BEEKEEPING TO HELP POLINATE THEIR GARDENS AND PROVIDE HONEY FOR THEIR HOME.

Polination

Bees help pollinate plants within a 2 mile or 3.2km radius.

Help Plants

Bees help plants produce fruit, flowers, nuts, and seeds.

Apiary

An apiary is where bee hives are kept, known as a bee yard.

Honey

Collecting honey is known as honey harvesting or honey extraction.

Nectar

Bees collect nectar from flowers and convert it to honey.

Beekeeping

Beekeeping, or apiculture, involves maintaining bee colonies in artificial beehives to collect honey and other hive products like beeswax, propolis, and bee pollen, while also supporting crop pollination. Beekeepers provide bees with shelter and resources, and intervene when necessary, such as adding or removing equipment or collecting swarms.

ANATOMY OF A BEE

LIFECYCLE OF THE BEE

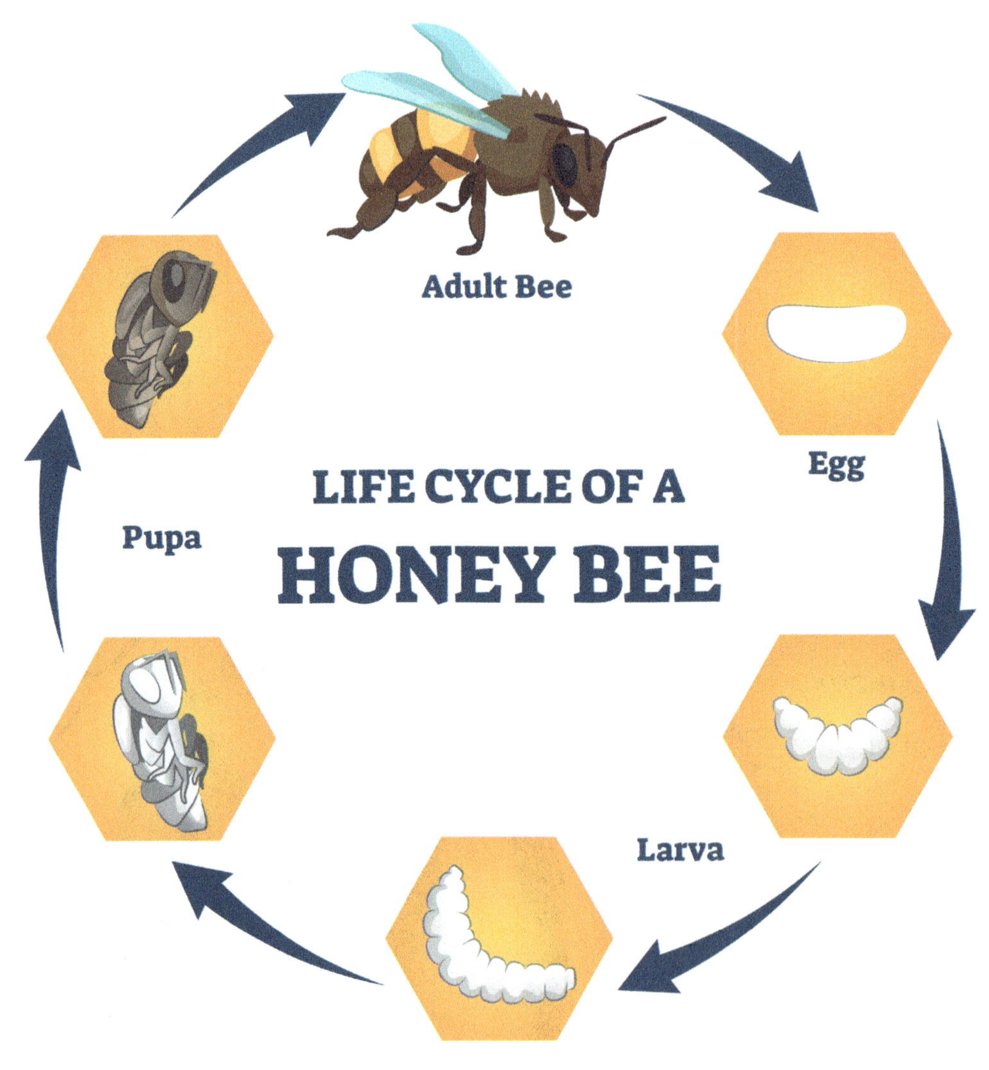

Bee Color by Number

Use the key at the bottom of the page to color the picture.

1. pink 2. brown 3. black
4. yellow 5. blue 6. green
7. purple

Directions: Fill in the boxes below to reflect on your learning today. What did you learn, and what questions do you still have?

3 THINGS I LEARNED

1.

2.

3.

2 INTERESTING FACTS

1.

2.

1 QUESTION I HAVE

1.

LADYBUG FACTS

THERE ARE 5000 DIFFERENT TYPES OF LADYBUGS IN THE WORLD

LADYBUGS LIVE 2-3 YEARS

ONE LADYBUG CAN EAT 5000 INSECTS IN ITS LIFETIME

FARMERS LOVE LADYBUGS BECAUSE THEY EAT APHIDS AND OTHER PLANT-EATING PESTS.

LADYBUGS LAY THEIR EGGS ON THE UNDERSIDE OF A LEAF IN CLUSTERS

LADYBUGS CAN HAVE STRIPES, SPOTS, OR NO MARKINGS AT ALL

THEY SECRETE AN OILY, FOUL-TASTING FLUID FROM THEIR LEGS TO WARD OFF PREDATORS

ANATOMY OF A LADYBUG

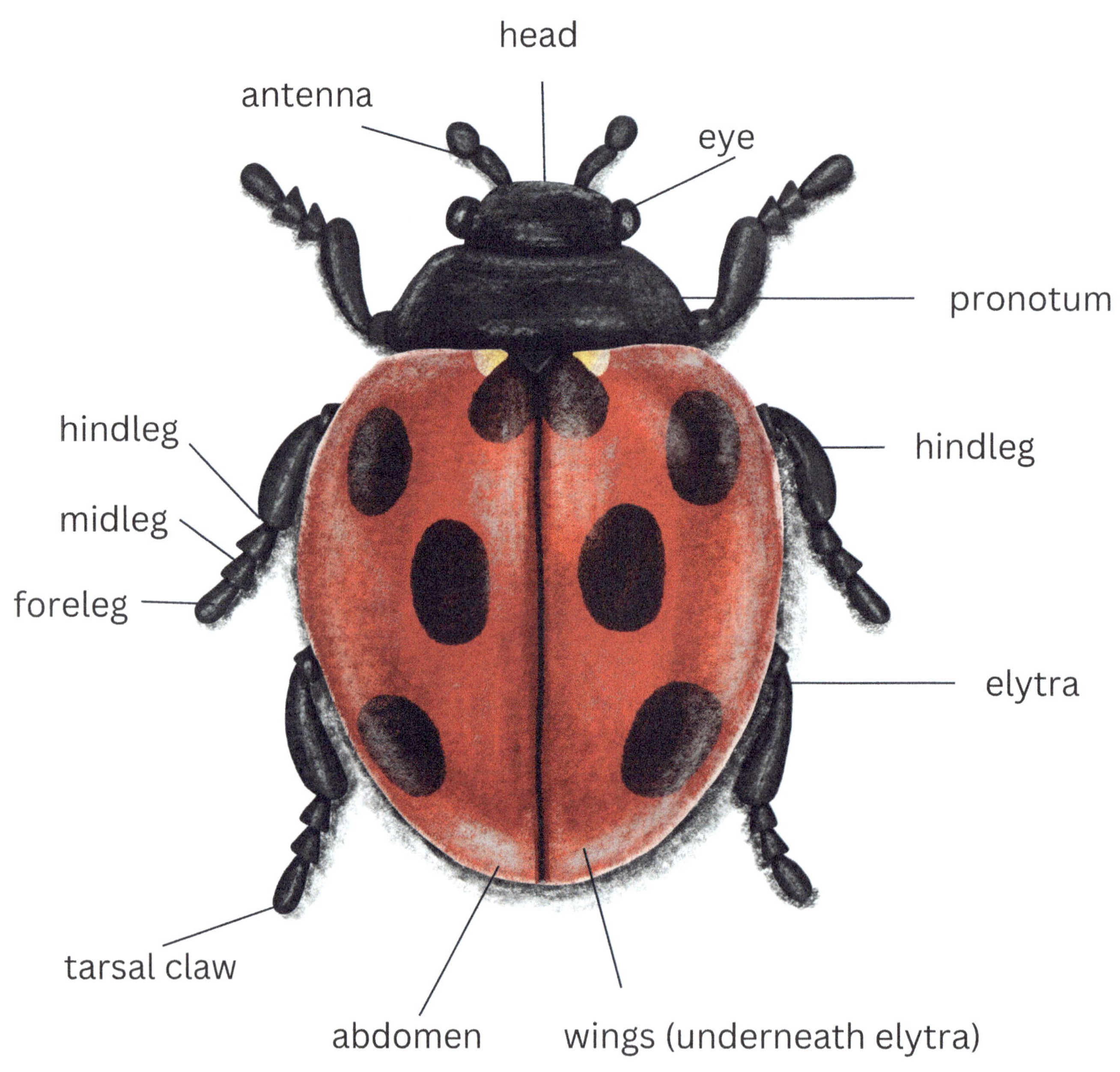

LIFE CYCLE:

ladybug

Research these the different stages of a ladybug's life:

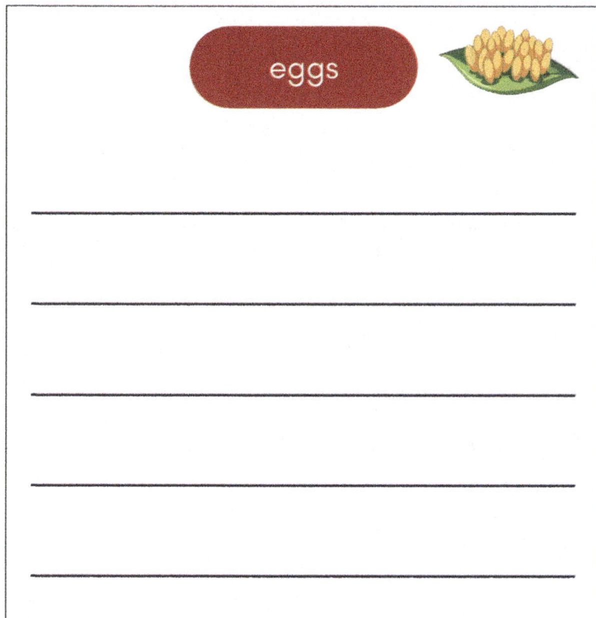

Name: Date:

INSECTS

WORD SEARCH

Can you find all the insect related words?

C	S	U	L	B	E	E	T	L	E	T	A
L	O	W	L	M	H	C	I	L	A	U	D
A	A	M	O	S	Q	U	I	T	O	L	R
D	W	C	A	R	O	Y	K	U	T	I	A
Y	F	C	O	T	M	E	A	I	S	C	G
B	A	R	C	F	F	O	C	A	S	K	O
U	B	I	A	N	L	H	T	G	N	E	N
G	I	C	I	Z	Z	Y	A	S	A	T	F
C	U	K	B	M	O	T	H	O	I	E	L
B	E	E	K	F	C	Y	C	M	L	I	Y
D	R	T	E	N	F	O	V	I	R	K	N
H	C	E	N	T	I	P	E	D	E	A	R

MOTH	LADYBUG	DRAGONFLY	ANT
SNAIL	BEETLE	MOSQUITO	FLY
WORM	CRICKET	CENTIPEDE	BEE

BUTTERFLY FACTS

BUTTERFLIES TASTE WITH THEIR FEET

BUTTERFLIES USE THE SUN TO NAVIGATE

A GROUP OF BUTTERFLIES IS CALLED A KALEIDESCOPE

BUTTERFLIES CAN FLY AS FAST AS 30MPH OR 48KM/HR

CATERPILLARS ARE BRIGHTLY COLORED TO WARN PREDATORS

BUTTERFLIES ARE IMPORTANT POLLINATORS

ENHANCE BIODIVERSITY AND ARE A SIGN OF A HEALTHY ENVIRONMENT

ANATOMY OF A BUTTERFLY

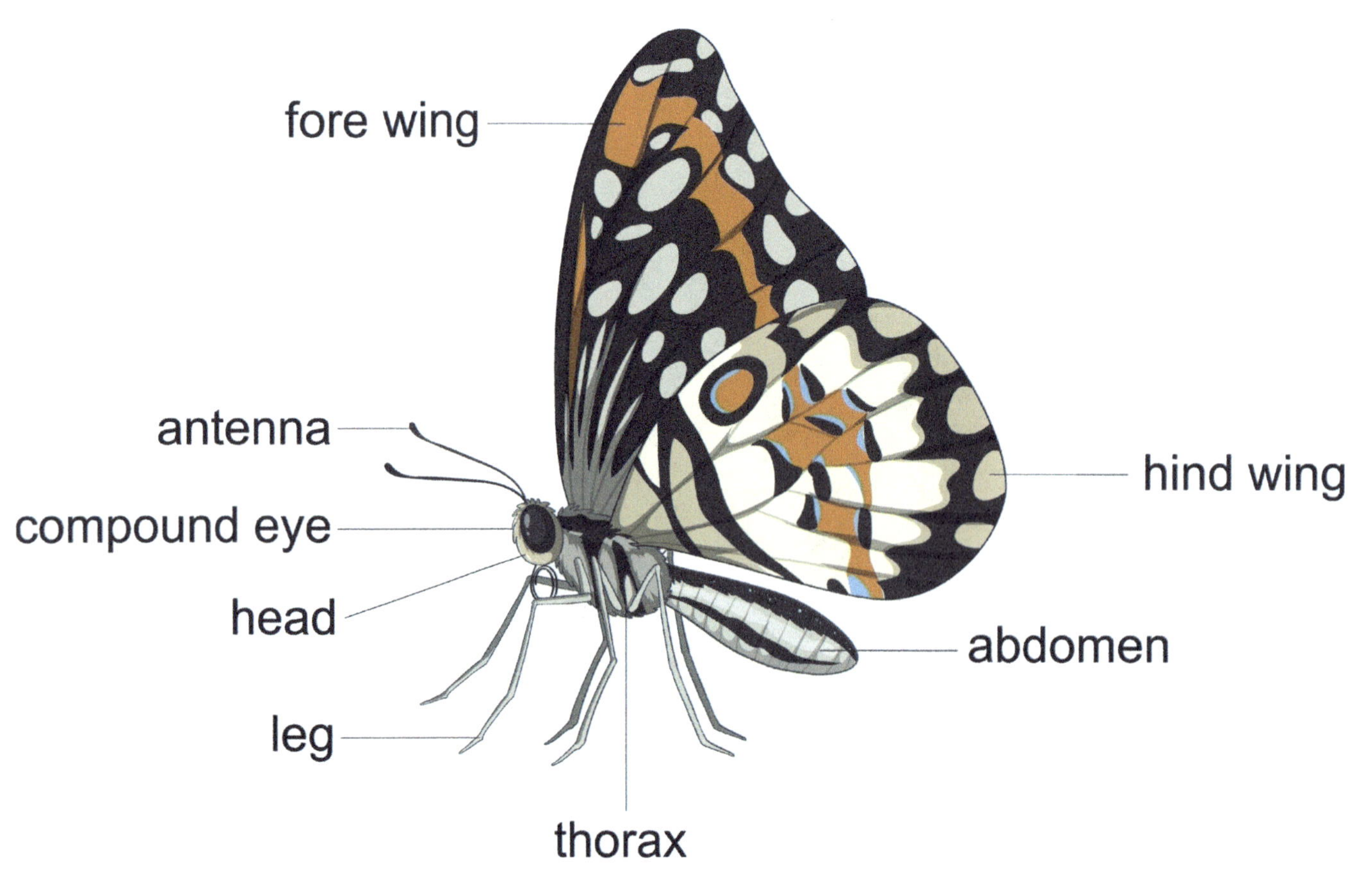

LIFE CYCLE OF THE BUTTERFLY

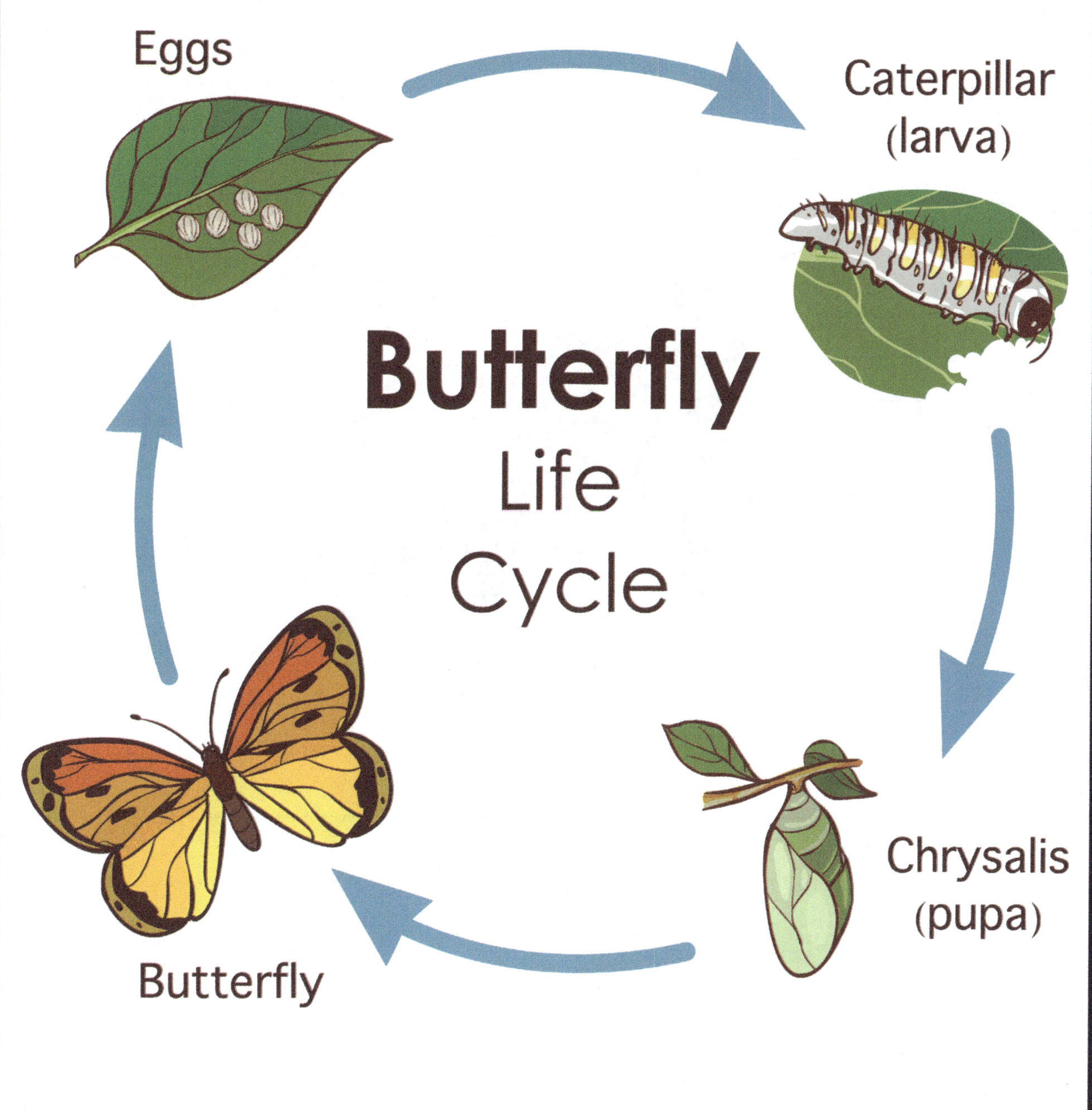

ANATOMY OF A BEE

Complete the bee anatomy for each part:

COLOR THE BUTTERFLY

ANATOMY OF A LADYBUG

Complete the ladybug anatomy for each part:

ANATOMY OF A BUTTERFLY

Complete the butterfly anatomy for each part:

LIFECYCLE OF THE BEE

Fill in the names of each stage of the bee life cycle:

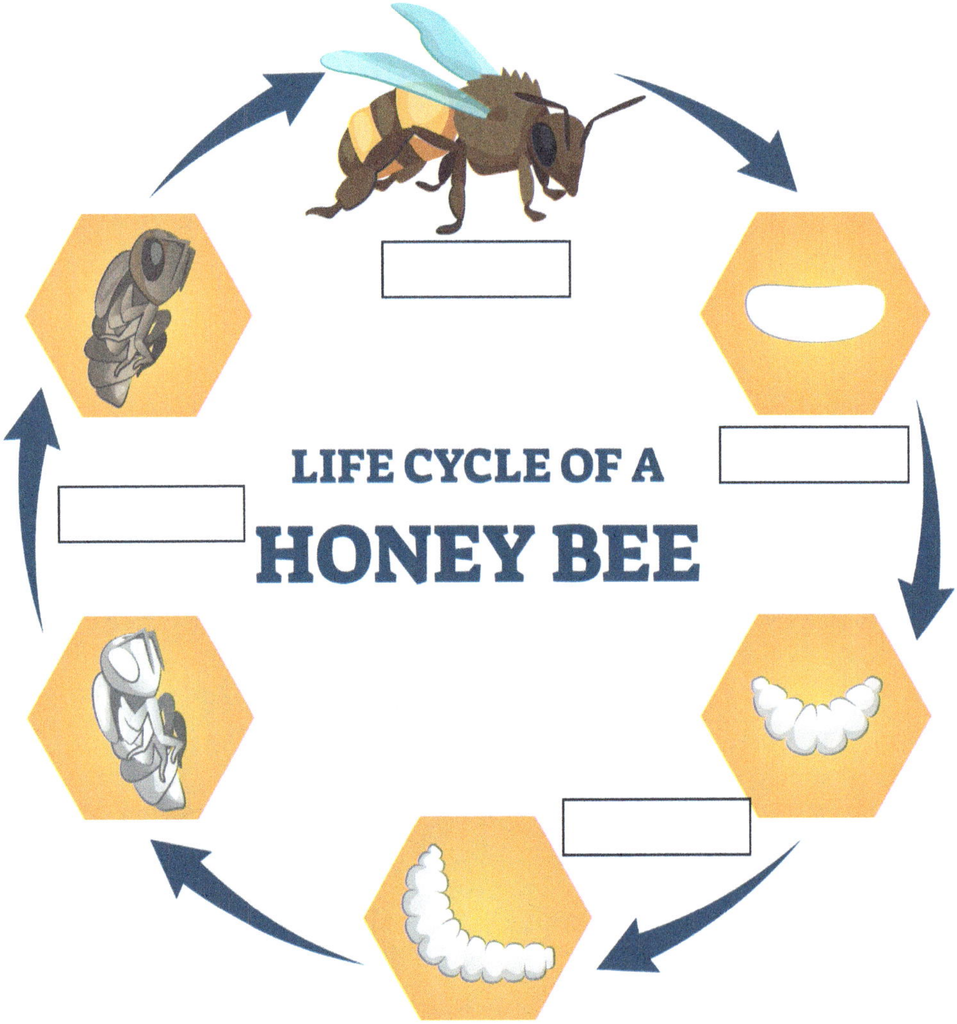

LIFE CYCLE OF A

HONEY BEE

Name: ______________________ Date: ____________________

All About Insects

Fill in the blanks below about insects using the words provided:

honey	leaves	drones	feet	aphids	chrysalis	pollinate
5000	larvae	pollinators	keleidescope	nectar	caterpillar	

1. Bees taste with their ____________ .
2. Bees collect ____________ from flowers and make ____________ .
3. Male bees are called ____________ .
4. Bees help ____________ plants within a 2 mile or 3.2 km radius.
5. A butterfly larvae is called a ______________ .
6. Butterflies are considered important ____________ .
7. When insect eggs hatch they are known as ____________ .
8. A butterfly pupa is also known as a ______________ .
9. A group of butterflies is called a ____________ .
10. Ladybugs eat ____________ and other pests.
11. A Ladybug eats ____________ insects in it's lifetime.
12. Ladybugs lay their eggs on the underside of ____________ in clusters.

Snapshots of

Bugs in my garden

Draw pictures of two bugs you might find in a garden. Name each bug and write a short description about what it looks like, its color, and where it lives.

PRESERVING FOOD

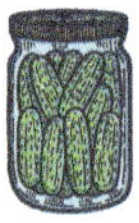

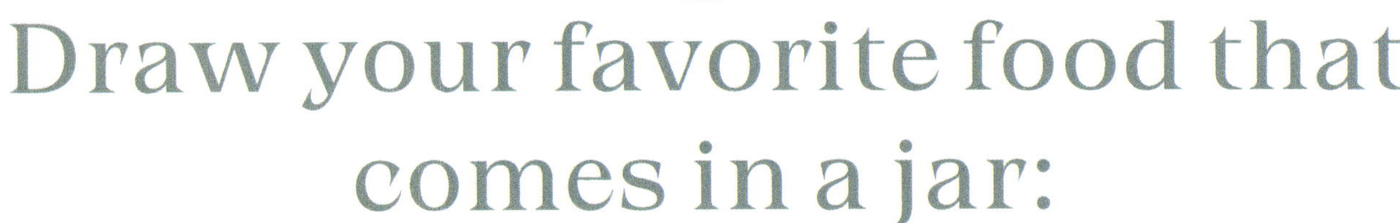

Draw your favorite food that comes in a jar:

DEER CREEK

HOMESTEAD

TYPES OF FOOD PRESERVATION

CANNING (WATER & PRESSURE)

WATERGLASSING

DEHYDRATING

FREEZE DRYING

FREEZING

PICKLING & SALTING

SMOKING

FERMENTATION

Write a Story

Write a story using these words:
canning, strawberries, chicken

CANNING

Determining which method of canning is best will depend on the acidity of the food. Acid can be added to change the acidity of a dish. The level of acidity determines the risk of becoming contaminated with botulism. Heat cannot kill botulism but acid can.

PRESSURE CANNING

Uses the heat of pure steam and pressure to seal jars airtight.

Requires a pressure canner.

Best for low acid foods such as meat and most vegetables (except tomatoes).

More acid (lemon, vinegar) can be added to make it higher in acid to water bath.

WATER BATH CANNING

Uses boiling water to create airtight seals in jars.

Requires a waterbath canner.

Boiling kills microorganisms (except botulism).

Best for high acid foods such as fruits, pickles, jams, and jellies, as well as tomatoes.

*Botulism is a rare but serious condition caused by a toxin that attacks the body's nerves. Botulism may cause life-threatening symptoms.

WATER GLASSING

Water glassing eggs is **a traditional method of preserving eggs using a solution of water and pickling lime (calcium hydroxide) to seal the eggshell and prevent spoilage for up to 12-18 months**, allowing you to enjoy fresh eggs year-round.

EGG STORAGE

Unwashed eggs with bloom on them can last at room temperature for roughly one month.

Refrigerated eggs with the bloom in tact can last for months.

Chickens often produce a lot of eggs in the summer and very few in the winter.

WATER GLASSING

To "water glass" eggs for long-term storage, mix one ounce of pickling lime with one quart of filtered water, then submerge unwashed eggs that are clean with no poop or debris in the solution, ensuring they are fully covered, and store them in a cool, dark place.

DEHYDRATING

Dehydrating food is a food preservation method where moisture is removed, extending shelf life by stopping microbes from growing. Dehydrated foods are smaller, lighter, and require no refrigeration, making them ideal for backpacking, hiking, and long-term storage.

NATURAL DEHYDRATION

Sun drying is a traditional method of dehydration. Food is exposed to sunlight and wind to evaporate moisture.

Foods can include meat, fruit, vegetables, grains, beans, herbs, and sauces.

Dehydrating is one of the oldest methods of food preservation and has been used effectively since the dawn of civilization.

ARTIFICIAL DEHYDRATION

Modern methods involve using food dehydrators or ovens with controlled temperatures and airflow to remove moisture efficiently.

While dehydration helps preserve food, it's important to ensure proper drying to prevent the growth of harmful bacteria, yeast, and mold.

FREEZE DRYING

Freeze drying is a dehydration process where water is removed from a product by freezing it and then sublimating the ice directly into vapor under a vacuum, preserving its original texture, flavor, and nutritional value.

FREEZING

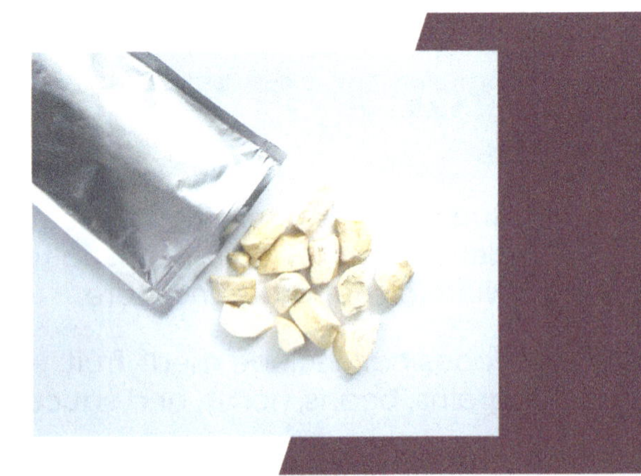

The material is first frozen to a very low temperature, forming ice crystals.

The frozen material is placed in a vacuum chamber, and the pressure is reduced, known as sublimation.

The low pressure, combined with a slight increase in temperature, allows the ice crystals to turn directly into water vapor (sublimate) without melting.

REHYDRATION

Once the material is dried, it can be rehydrated, and it will retain many of its original qualities, including shape, structure, and nutrients.

Freeze drying is used for preserving food, biological materials, pharmaceuticals, and other products

Sublimation is the process where water transitions directly from a solid (ice) to a gas (vapor) without passing through the liquid phase

SMOKING

Food smoking is a cooking and preservation method that involves exposing food, particularly meat, fish, and cheese, to smoke from burning or smoldering material, most often wood, to impart flavor, color, and a degree of preservation.

SMOKING PROCESS

Before cold smoking, foods, especially meats, are often cured, which involves adding salt and other ingredients to enhance preservation and flavor.

Smoke acts as a natural preservative.

Smoking can alter the texture of food, making it more tender, and can also lead to a rich brown color.

The smoke's drying effect and certain chemicals (like formaldehyde and alcohols) help preserve food by inhibiting bacterial growth and slowing down fat oxidation.

Hot smoking involves cooking the food at the same time as smoking, while cold smoking focuses more on flavor and preservation without cooking.

Fermentation in food preservation is a metabolic, natural process where microorganisms, like bacteria and yeast, break down carbohydrates (like sugars) into acids, gases, or alcohol, creating an environment that inhibits the growth of harmful bacteria and extends the shelf life of food.

FERMENTATION PROCESS

Lactic acid fermentation: Used in the production of yogurt, sauerkraut, and kimchi, where lactic acid bacteria convert sugars into lactic acid, which acidifies the food and inhibits the growth of spoilage microorganisms.
Alcoholic fermentation: Used in the production of wine, beer, and bread, where yeast converts sugars into alcohol and carbon dioxide.
Acetic acid fermentation: Used in the production of vinegar, where bacteria convert alcohol into acetic acid.

FERMENTED FOODS

Fermented foods include yogurt, cheese, kimchi, sauerkraut, kombucha, tempeh, and bread (if made with yeast).

Fermentation can enhance the nutritional value of food by increasing the availability of certain vitamins and minerals, and it can also make nutrients more easily digestible.

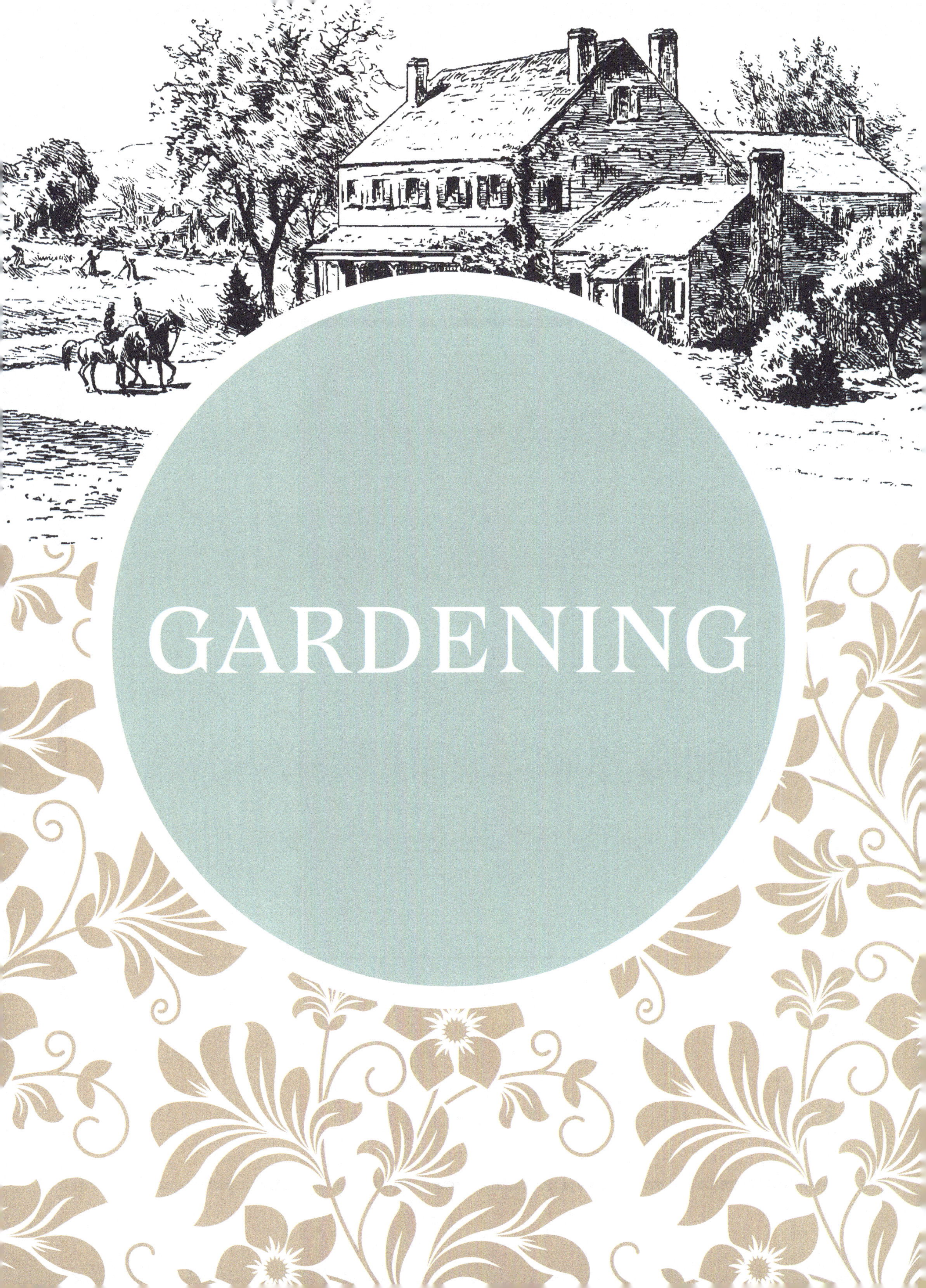

GARDENING

Draw your favorite plant (fruit, vegetable, flower):

DEER CREEK

HOMESTEAD

THINGS YOU CAN GROW FROM HOME

FRUITS

VEGETABLES

HERBS

FRUIT TREES

NUTS

GRAINS

FLOWERS

PLANTS TO HELP OTHER PLANTS

THINGS TO KNOW BEFORE STARTING YOUR GARDEN

FIND THE SUNNIEST SPOT. MOST EDIBLE PLANTS NEED FULL SUN TO THRIVE. FULL SUN IS 6 OR MORE DIRECT HOURS OF SUNLIGHT.

MAKE A WATERING PLAN. RAIN IS GREAT BUT NOT ALWAYS RELIABLE. HAVE AN ALTERNATE PLAN. DON'T WATER DURING THE HOTTEST PART OF THE DAY.

TEST YOUR SOIL AND ADD NUTRIENTS IF NEEDED. THIS IS NOT NEEDED IF USING RAISED BED AND POTTED SOIL.

GROW WHAT YOU'LL EAT. DON'T GROW VEGETABLES YOU DON'T LIKE OR WON'T EAT.

INSPECT YOUR GARDEN OFTEN. REMOVE WEEDS, CHECK FOR BUGS, MAKE SURE THE PLANTS HAVE ENOUGH WATER, AND CHECK FOR DISEASE.

MICROGREENS

MICROGREENS OFFER NUMEROUS HEALTH BENEFITS, INCLUDING A HIGHER CONCENTRATION OF VITAMINS, MINERALS, AND ANTIOXIDANTS COMPARED TO THEIR MATURE COUNTERPARTS, SUPPORTING SKIN HEALTH, DIGESTION, AND POTENTIALLY REDUCING THE RISK OF CERTAIN DISEASES. THEY ALSO PROMOTE A HEALTHY IMMUNE SYSTEM AND CAN BE A SUSTAINABLE FOOD CHOICE.

Microgreens are a nutritional powerhouse!

Salad greens, leafy vegetables, herbs and even edible flowers can be grown as microgreens, though some varieties are better suited than others. Beginners often start by growing one type of seed, such as broccoli, cauliflower, cabbage, mustard, chia, sunflower or buckwheat — among the easiest-to-grow varieties of microgreens.

Start with a warm, sunny windowsill (direct sunlight from a south-facing window is ideal) and a small, clean container. Plastic take-out dishes and disposable pie plates work well, as do clear fruit or salad boxes. If your chosen container doesn't have built-in drainage, poke a few drainage holes in the bottom. Then, prepare to plant:

Add 1-2 inches of moistened potting soil to the bottom of the container. Sprinkle seeds all over and press lightly. Cover with a thin layer of potting soil. Dappen with a mister. Cover with a clear lid or plastic wrap for 3-7 days or until spouted. Remove lid and continue to mist twice a day. Plants are ready to harvest when true leaves form, roughly 2 inches tall. Use sissors to trim right to soil level.

Life Cyle of the Plant

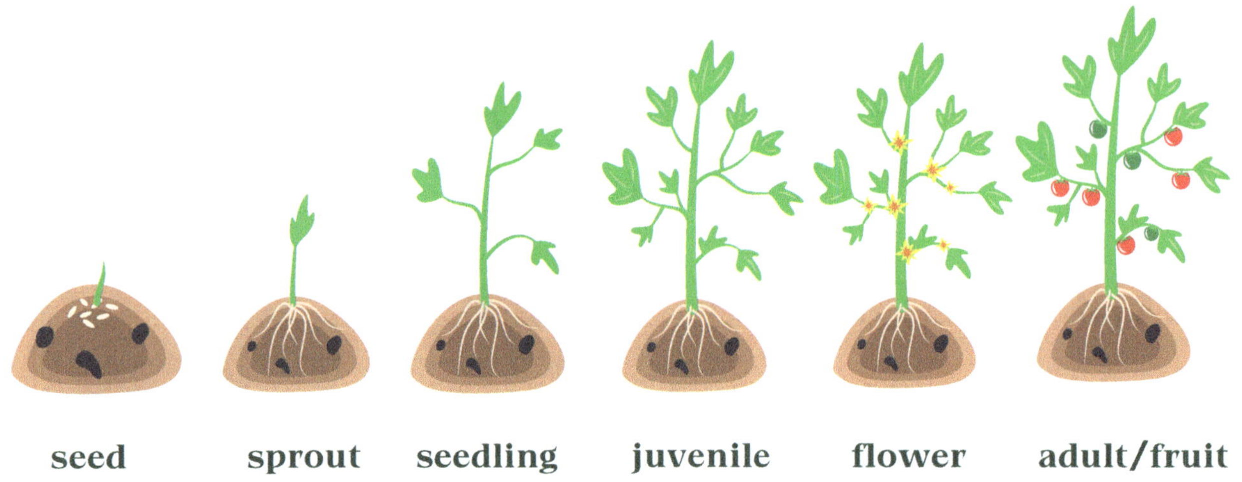

Plant Hardiness Zones

A plant hardiness zone is a geographic area defined by its average annual minimum temperature, which helps gardeners and landscapers understand which plants are likely to thrive in a specific climate.

It is important to choose seeds based on the zone you live in. Some plants, such as oranges, can only survive in really warm climates. Other plants do well in colder climates, such as carrots, spinach, and peonies!

Homesteaders who want to plant seeds outside of their zone must rely on the use of external supports, such as greenhouses, indoor growing lights, or tarps/blankets outside through the winter.

The United States Department of Agriculture (USDA) developed a plant hardiness zone map, which divides North America into 13 zones based on average annual minimum temperatures. Canada also uses a similar system, with zones ranging from 0 (coldest) to 9(warmest).

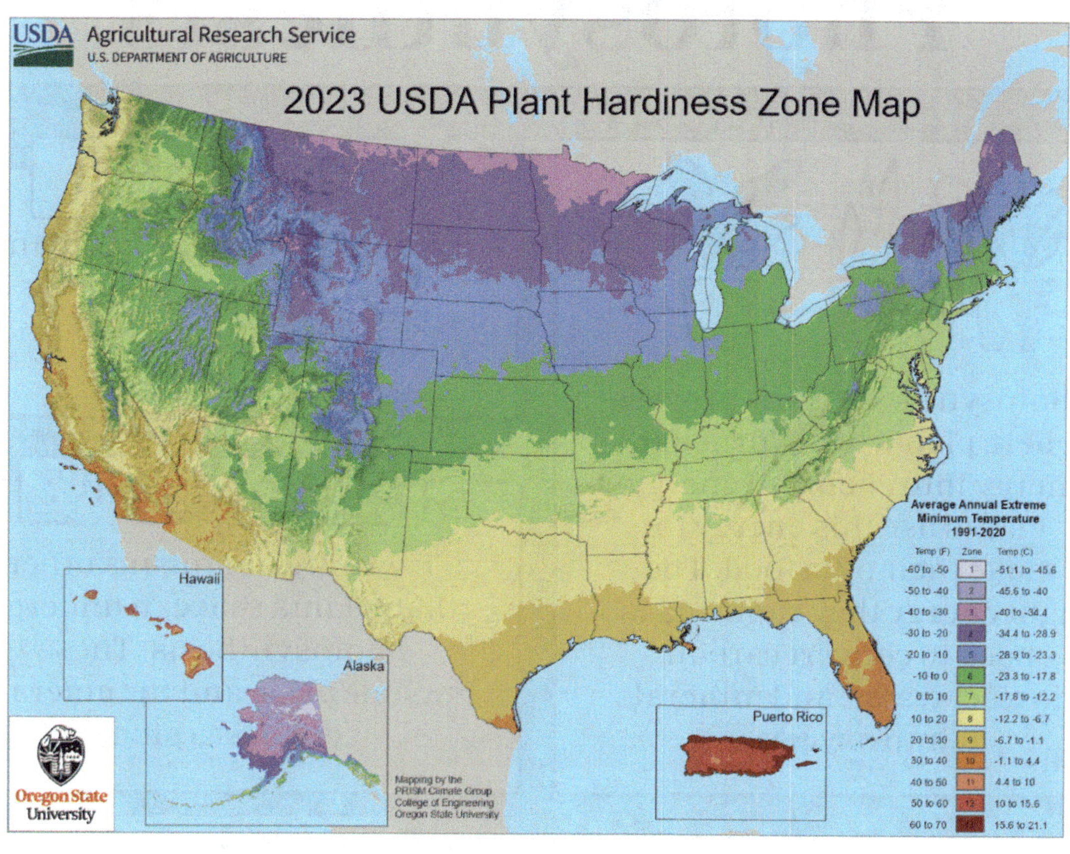
USDA Agricultural Research Service
U.S. DEPARTMENT OF AGRICULTURE
2023 USDA Plant Hardiness Zone Map
Hawaii
Alaska
Puerto Rico
Oregon State University
Mapping by the PRISM Climate Group College of Engineering Oregon State University
Average Annual Extreme Minimum Temperature 1991-2020
Temp (F) Zone Temp (C)
-60 to -50 1 -51.1 to -45.6
-50 to -40 2 -45.6 to -40
-40 to -30 3 -40 to -34.4
-30 to -20 4 -34.4 to -28.9
-20 to -10 5 -28.9 to -23.3
-10 to 0 6 -23.3 to -17.8
0 to 10 7 -17.8 to -12.2
10 to 20 8 -12.2 to -6.7
20 to 30 9 -6.7 to -1.1
30 to 40 10 -1.1 to 4.4
40 to 50 11 4.4 to 10
50 to 60 12 10 to 15.6
60 to 70 13 15.6 to 21.1

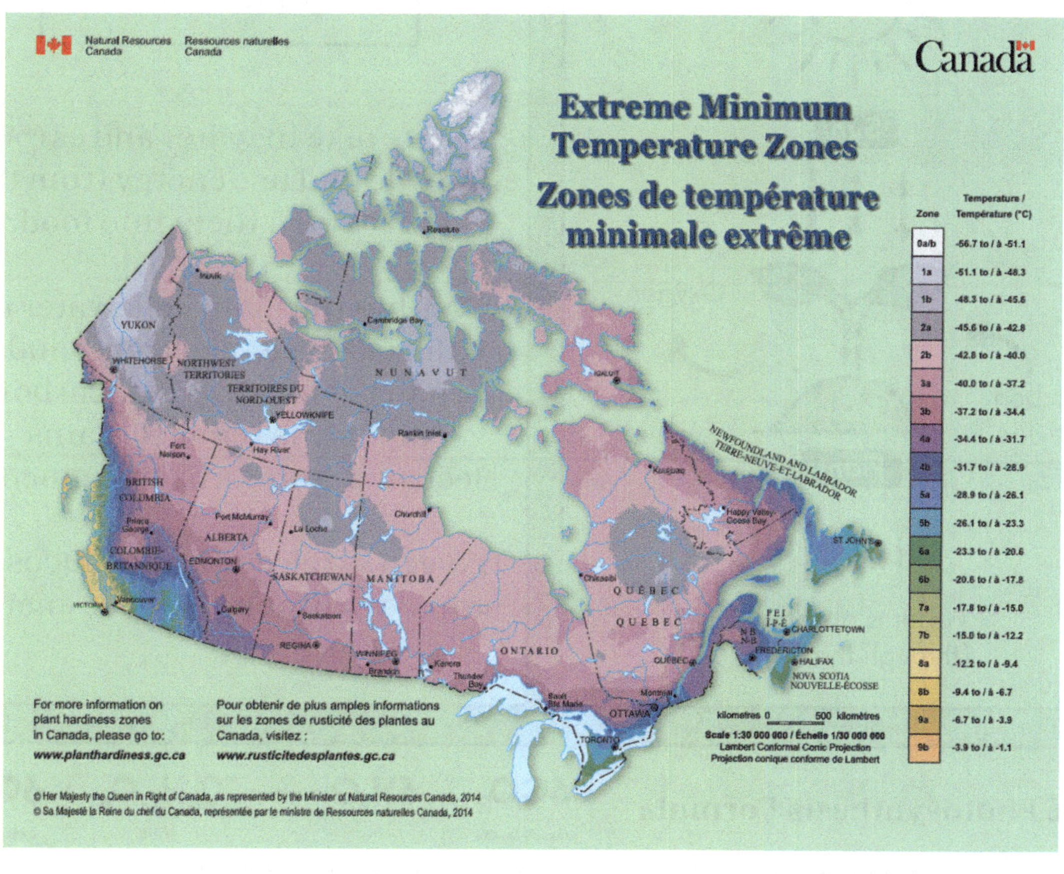
Natural Resources Canada
Ressources naturelles Canada
Canada
Extreme Minimum Temperature Zones
Zones de température minimale extrême
Zone
Temperature / Température (°C)
0a/b -56.7 to / à -51.1
1a -51.1 to / à -48.3
1b -48.3 to / à -45.6
2a -45.6 to / à -42.8
2b -42.8 to / à -40.0
3a -40.0 to / à -37.2
3b -37.2 to / à -34.4
4a -34.4 to / à -31.7
4b -31.7 to / à -28.9
5a -28.9 to / à -26.1
5b -26.1 to / à -23.3
6a -23.3 to / à -20.6
6b -20.6 to / à -17.8
7a -17.8 to / à -15.0
7b -15.0 to / à -12.2
8a -12.2 to / à -9.4
8b -9.4 to / à -6.7
9a -6.7 to / à -3.9
9b -3.9 to / à -1.1
YUKON
WHITEHORSE
NORTHWEST TERRITORIES
TERRITOIRES DU NORD-OUEST
YELLOWKNIFE
NUNAVUT
BRITISH COLUMBIA
COLOMBIE-BRITANNIQUE
ALBERTA
EDMONTON
SASKATCHEWAN
MANITOBA
ONTARIO
QUÉBEC
QUEBEC
OTTAWA
TORONTO
NEWFOUNDLAND AND LABRADOR
TERRE-NEUVE-ET-LABRADOR
ST JOHN'S
CHARLOTTETOWN
FREDERICTON
HALIFAX
NOVA SCOTIA
NOUVELLE-ÉCOSSE
For more information on plant hardiness zones in Canada, please go to:
www.planthardiness.gc.ca
Pour obtenir de plus amples informations sur les zones de rusticité des plantes au Canada, visitez :
www.rusticitedesplantes.gc.ca
kilometres 0 500 kilomètres
Scale 1:30 000 000 / Échelle 1/30 000 000
Lambert Conformal Conic Projection
Projection conique conforme de Lambert
© Her Majesty the Queen in Right of Canada, as represented by the Minister of Natural Resources Canada, 2014
© Sa Majesté la Reine du chef du Canada, représentée par le ministre de Ressources naturelles Canada, 2014

Photosynthesis

Photosynthesis is the process where plants transform light energy into chemical energy. Plants use this energy to make their own food. The light energy they captured is used to convert carbon dioxide, water, and minerals into oxygen.

Chlorophyll

The pigment that gives plants their green color and helps in the process of photosynthesis.

Did you know?

There are organisms other than plants that can undergo photosynthesis. These include algae and the emerald green sea slug.

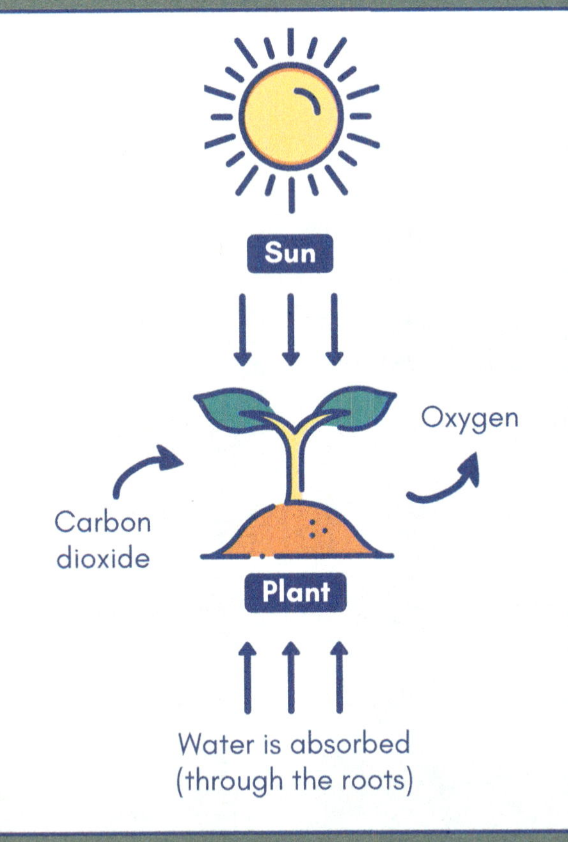

The Photosynthesis Process

Plants take in water and carbon dioxide and use energy from the sun to turn them into food.

Within the plant cell, water is oxidized, loses electrons, and is changed into oxygen. Carbon dioxide is reduced, gains electrons, and turns into glucose.

Oxygen is released, and glucose is stored within the plant as energy.

The Photosynthesis Formula

$$6CO_2 + 6H_2O \longrightarrow C_6H_{12}O_6 + 6O^2$$

CARBON DIOXIDE, WATER, SUGAR, OXYGEN

SOURCES: ENCYCLOPEDIA BRITANNICA, NATIONAL GEOGRAPHIC

Plant Hardiness Zones

What plant hardiness zone do you live in?

List some seeds you can grow where you live:

Describe why a greenhouse could allow you to plant seeds from a warmer zone?

CROSSWORD PUZZLE

Name: ____________________

Class: ____________________

Fruits

- Fill in the crossword puzzle below with the names of fruits.

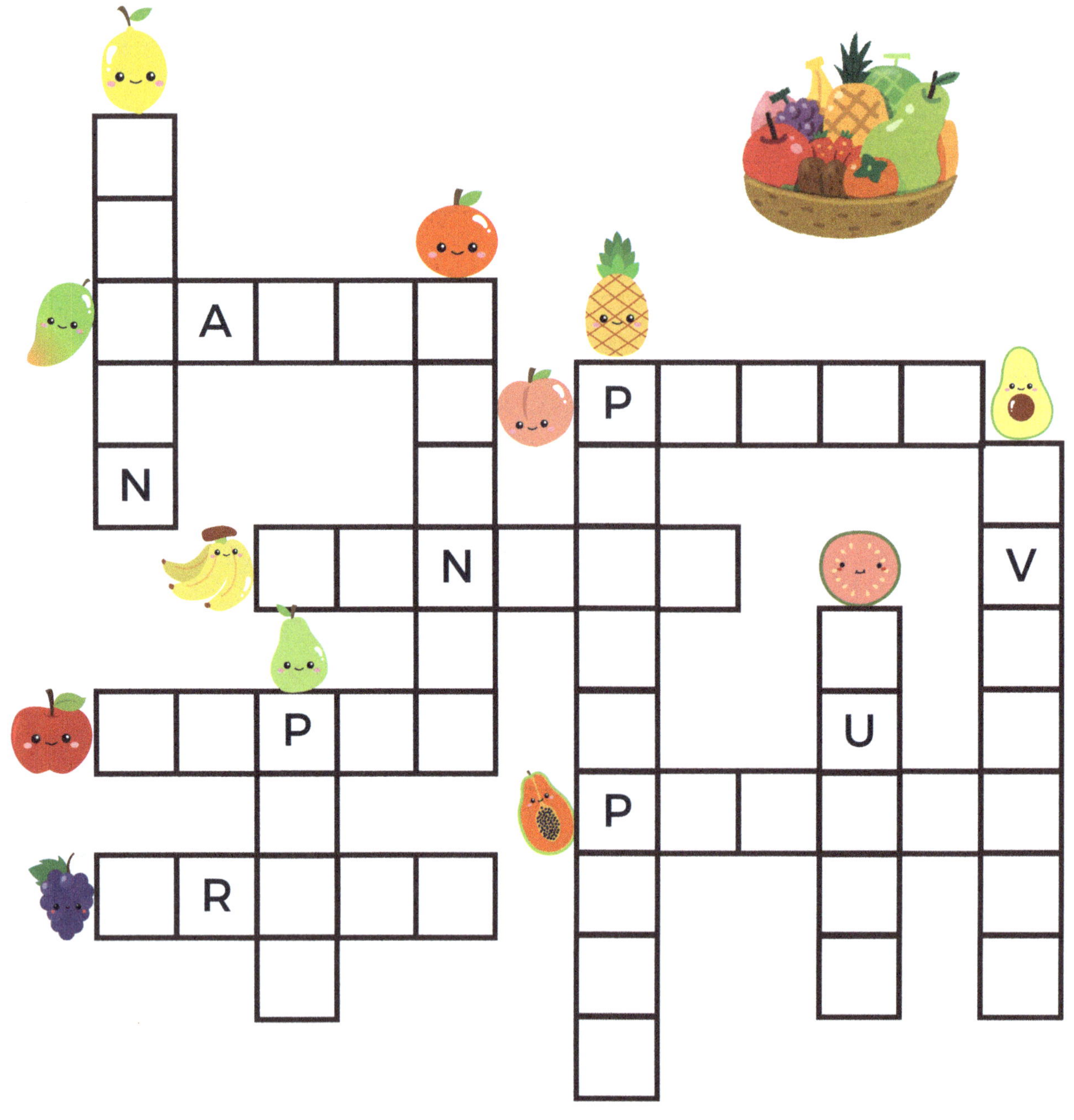

WHEAT FACTS

WHEAT BERRIES HAVE AN VERY LONG SHELF LIFE. THEY HAVE BEEN FOUND IN THE PYRAMIDS STILL FRESH!

STORE BOUGHT FLOUR HAS A SHELF LIFE OF 6-8 MONTHS

FRESH GROUND WHEAT HAS NATURAL B VITAMINS

WHITE FLOUR HAS THE FIBRES, VITAMINS AND MINERALS STRIPPED AWAY

WHITE FLOUR HAS PRESERVATIVES AND IS OFTEN BLEACHED

WHOLE GRAINS REDUCE THE RISK OF DIABETES, HEART DISEASE, CANCER, STROKE, & OBESITY.

MILLED WHEAT *MAY* BE TOLLERABLE FOR THOSE WHO ARE GLUTEN INTOLLERANT

WHEAT

THE WHEAT KERNEL, ALSO KNOWN AS THE WHEAT BERRY, IS A WHOLE GRAIN THAT CONTAINS ESSENTIAL NUTRIENTS IMPORTANT FOR OUR BODIES.

ANATOMY OF A GRAIN

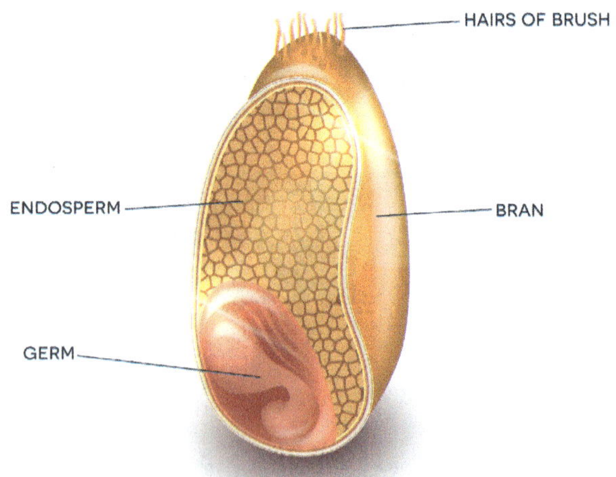

Germ is the nutrient-packed powerhouse found at the end of the kernel. Wheat germ is a rich, concentrated source of saturated fats, plant sterols, antioxidants, vitamin A, vitamin E, iron, folate, thiamin, riboflavin, calcium, phosphorous and magnesium.

BRAN: Bran makes up about 14.5% of the kernel weight. Bran is can be included in whole wheat flour and can also be bought separately. The bran contains a small amount of protein, large amounts of B-vitamins, trace minerals, and dietary fibre - primarily insoluable.

ENDOSPERM: Makes up about 83% of the kernel weight and is the source of white flour. The endosperm contains the greatest source of protein, carbohydrates, and iron. It also contains major B-vitamins such as riboflavin, niacin, and thiamine. It is also a source of soluable fibre.

GERM: Makes up 2.5% of kernel weight. The germ is the sprouting section of the seed. It contains minimal quantities of high quality proteins and a greater share of B-complex vitamins and trace minerals. It can be purchased separately and is part of whole wheat flour.

Name: Date:

WHEAT

WORD SEARCH

Can you find all the wheat related words?

C	L	E	F	O	R	A	S	I	Z	Z	A
B	E	R	R	Y	I	L	L	N	Y	A	I
S	Q	B	E	R	N	I	E	T	O	R	P
T	W	I	N	O	P	G	N	M	R	A	E
N	H	F	L	S	L	A	R	E	N	I	M
E	E	F	A	M	W	E	E	D	T	R	R
I	A	T	E	L	P	I	K	F	E	W	E
R	T	O	A	S	T	C	C	G	I	H	A
T	O	T	O	O	G	B	N	H	N	O	M
U	T	D	E	U	F	L	O	U	R	L	O
N	N	I	N	P	E	O	R	A	N	E	E
E	H	N	A	R	B	A	T	E	R	I	Y

WHEAT	GERM	NUTRIENTS	MINERALS
WHOLE	ENDOSPERM	FLOUR	KERNEL
BERRY	BRAN	PROTEIN	FIBRE

Name: ______________________ Date: ______________________

All About Gardening

Fill in the blanks below about gardening using the words provided:

oxygen	berries	chlorophyll	powerhouse	pyramids	photosynthesis
zone	climates	sun	hottest	endosperm	carbon dioxide	antioxidants

1. Most plants need full ______________ to survive.
2. Plants take in ______________ and turn it into ______________ .
3. Plants can only survive in certain ______________ .
4. Wheat kernels are also known as wheat ______________ .
5. Wheat berries have been found in the ______________ .
6. Wheat is made up of the germ, bran, and ______________ .
7. The pigment that gives plants their green color is called ______________ .
8. ______________ is the process where plants turn light into energy.
9. A plant hardiness ______________ details the average minimum temperature.
10. Don't water your garden during the ______________ part of the day.
11. Germ is the nutrient packed ______________ .
12. Microgreens contain a higher concentration of ______________ minerals, and vitamins.

HANDMADE

Draw your favorite thing to make with items from home:

CRAFTING

CRAFTING IS AN IMPORTANT WAY FOR HOMESTEADERS TO STAY SELF-SUFFICIENT. THIS MAY INCLUDE SEWING, KNITTING, WOODWORKING, CERAMICS, AND ANY OTHER METHOD OF MAKING YOUR OWN PRODUCTS.

MAKING YOUR OWN PRODUCTS CAN REDUCE COST, ALLOW A PERSON TO CONTROL INGREDIENTS/REDUCE TOXIC CHEMICALS, UTILIZE MATERIALS MADE ON THEIR HOMESTEAD, AND HELP TOWARDS SELF-SUSTAINABILITY.

SEWING/KNITTING/CROCHETING: Homesteaders may utilize sewing to make their own clothes, curtains, bedding, and linens.

WOODWORKING: Woodworking is an important skill to have on a homestead. This skill can be used outside for building barns, fences, and garden beds, or inside for furniture, shelves, and tools. It can also be used to carve decoration and other daily tools.

CERAMICS: Learn how to make ceramics might include using a pottery wheel or molding clay with your hands to make bowls, plates, mugs, and decorations.

OTHER CRAFTS: Other crafts may include making candles, soap, laundry detergent, beauty products, cleaning supplies and more!

WOOL PROCESSING

PROCESSING WOOL INVOLVES THE STEPS TO GET THE WOOL OFF A SHEEP (OR OTHER ANIMALS), CLEANING IT, AND TURNING IT INTO YARN TO USE FOR PROJECTS.

Wool is primarily obtained from sheep, but other animals like goats, rabbits, alpacas, and even camels, yaks, and musk oxen, also produce fibers that can be called "wool".

SHEARING: The fleece is removed from the sheep, often with specialized shears and then is washed.

SKIRTING: This involves removing any unwanted parts of the fleece, such as matted wool, dirt, or vegetation.

SCOURING: The fleece is washed to remove dirt, grease, and other impurities.

SORTING: The wool is then sorted by quality, length, and color.

CARDING: This process untangles and aligns the wool fibers, preparing them for spinning.

COMBING: This step further aligns the fibers and removes any remaining short or uneven fibers, resulting in a higher quality, cleaner wool for worsted yarn.

SPINNING: The carded or combed wool is then spun into yarn, either by hand using a spinning wheel or spindle, or mechanically.

DYING: The yarn can be dyed with natural or synthetic dyes to create a variety of colors.

BEESWAX CANDLES

Quick and Easy!

SERVINGS: 1 CANDLE　　PREPPING TIME: 5 MIN　　COOKING TIME: N/A

MATERIALS

beeswax sheets.
cotton wicks
blowdryer or heat gun
essential oils (optional)
cookie cutters (optional)

DIRECTIONS

1. Lay out one beeswax sheet of desired size.
2. Cut your wick to desired length. It should fit the length of the beeswax sheet with a bit extra to hang out the end.
3. If using essential oils, soak the wick in essential oil to give off a fragrant smell while burning.
4. Use a blowdryer or heat gun to gently warm the sheet up to make it easier to roll. Do not melt the wax, just warm for a few seconds.
5. Place the wick along one edge of the beeswax sheet and gently roll the wax up with the wick inside.
6. Use the heat gun to gently warm the seem and press down firmly.
7. If you want your candle thicker, simply roll your candle inside another sheet and use the heat gun to adhere.
8. You can use cookie cutters to cut out shapes and add onto the candle as decoration. Gently heat the candle and shapes then press firmly against the candle to apply.

ALL-PURPOSE CLEANER

Quick and Easy!

OPTION 1

MATERIALS

1 1/4 cups distilled water (this extends shelf life)
1/2 cup distilled white vinegar
10 drops essential oils

DIRECTIONS

1. Add all ingredients to a spray bottle. Shake and it is ready to use!

OPTION 2

MATERIALS

Several orange or lemon peels
Distilled white vinegar

DIRECTIONS

1. Place the peels into a glass mason jar. Fill to the top with the vinegar. Let it infuse for 3-4 weeks in a cool, dark place.
2. Strain the vinegar into a spray bottle and it is ready to use!

LAUNDRY DETERGENT

Quick and Easy!

SERVINGS: 50-60 WASHES PREPPING TIME: 10 MIN COOKING TIME: N/A

MATERIALS

1 cup washing soda
1 cup borax
1/2 cup baking soda
1/2 cup epsom salt
optional: 1 bar of grated castile soap
30 drops of essential oil
*make sure oils are child safe

DIRECTIONS

1. In a large bowl, combine the washing soda, borax, baking soda, and epsom salt. If you're using grated soap, add this as well.
2. Once your dry ingredients are well blended, add about 30 drops of essential oils (such as citrus or lavender). Start by mixing in small batches to ensure the oil is evenly distributed. Essential oils are great for adding a lovely scent, as well as for their antibacterial properties!
3. Transfer your detergent to an airtight container. This will help keep moisture out and preserve the essential oil scents.

HOW TO USE

1. For regular loads, use 1-2 tbsp of your homade detergent and add directly into your load. For larger or more soiled loads, use 2-3 tbsp.

Tips: Use hot water when using the grated soap version, and add a little extra borax if you have hard water to improve cleaning capabilities.

SIMMER POT POTPOURRI

Quick and Easy!

SERVING SIZE: 1 POT | PREPPING TIME: 5 MIN | COOKING TIME: 5 HRS

MATERIALS CHOOSE YOUR FRAGERENCE

Vanilla & Lavender: vanilla beans, dried lavender, lemon peel or dried slices

Cranberry Bliss: Fresh/dried cranberries, orange slices, cinnamon sticks

Forest Retreat: Pine sprigs, cedar chips, bay leaves

Apple Cinnamon Spice: Apple slices, cinnamon sticks, cloves, star anise

Cinnamon Orange Clove Blend: Cinnamon sticks, dried orange peel, cloves

Winter Woods & Spice: Juniper berries, pine needles, cinnamon, bay leaves

Apple & Eucalyptus Refresh: Apple slices, eucalyptus leavesm rosemary sprigs

Rosemary Citrus Fusion: Rosemary sprigs, lemon slices, thyme

DIRECTIONS

1. Add all ingredients into a large pot filled with water. bring water to simmer and let it remain simmering while fresh fragerance fills your home!

*Tips: You can let simmer pots cook for several hours. Be sure to check water levels and make sure it doesn't become dry. Reuse the simmer pot ingredients by putting them in the fridge for up to one week and put back into simmering water.

SELF-SUSTAINABILITY

Draw a renewable source of energy:

4 ways to Maintain Soil Fertility

01 Enrich the Soil with Organic Matter

Using compost, green manure, or other organic fertilizer can increase the organic matter content in the soil which is important for soil fertility.

02 Crop Rotation

Crop rotation helps prevent a decrease in soil fertility by avoiding the build up of soil diseases and balancing the nutrients used by different types of plants.

03 Conservation Farming

Methods such as tiered planting, row cropping, or no-till farming can help maintain soil structure and reduce erosion.

04 Proper Irrigation

Providing water in the right way and at the right time will help maintain soil moisture.

Your Dream Homestead

Imagine you had your own homestead. Answer below what it might look like:

1. Tell me where your homestead would be:

____

____

____

2. Tell me what animals you would have on your homestead:

____

____

3. Tell me what crafts you would like to learn how to do:

____

4. What fruits and vegetables would you hope to plant?

____

____

____

DEER CREEK

HOMESTEAD

THINGS YOU CAN DO TO BE SELF-SUSTAINABLE

USE SOLAR OR WIND POWER (RENEWABLE ENERGY)

RAINWATER HARVESTING

COMPOST

GARDENING

ANIMAL HUSBANDRY

FOOD PRESERVATION

INSECT FARMING

WASTE REDUCTION (REDUCE, REUSE, RECYCLE)

SELF-SUSTAINABILITY

ON A HOMESTEAD, SELF-SUSTAINABILITY MEANS PRODUCING AS MUCH AS POSSIBLE OF WHAT YOU NEED TO LIVE, FROM FOOD AND ENERGY TO RESOURCES LIKE WATER AND BUILDING MATERIALS, REDUCING RELIANCE ON EXTERNAL SYSTEMS AND RESOURCES.

SOLAR OR WIND POWER: These renewable energy sources allow a homestead to not rely on city electricity for power.

COMPOSTING: Composting allows scraps of food, lawn and garden debris, and other items from the homestead to be recycled and turned into nutrient-rich soil for the garden.

RAINWATER HARVESTING: Collecting rainwater allows homesteads to have water for their farm animals and gardens without worrying about droughts or water restrictions.

WOOD BURNING STOVE: Wood burning stoves rely on wood and can eliminate the need for furnaces, gas, and electricity for heating the home and even cooking!

MAKING YOUR OWN PRODUCTS CAN REDUCE COST, ALLOW A PERSON TO CONTROL INGREDIENTS/REDUCE TOXIC CHEMICALS, UTILIZE MATERIALS MADE ON THEIR HOMESTEAD, AND HELP TOWARDS SELF-SUSTAINABILITY.

COMPOSTING

COMPOSTING IS A NATURAL PROCESS WHERE MICROORGANISMS, LIKE BACTERIA AND FUNGI, BREAK DOWN ORGANIC MATERIALS (FOOD SCRAPS, YARD WASTE) INTO A NUTRIENT-RICH SOIL AMENDMENT CALLED COMPOST, WHICH ENRICHES SOIL AND SUPPORTS PLANT GROWTH.

Composting reduces waste, enriches soil, improves water retention, and can help control weeds.

COMPOSTING METHODS: You can compost in bins, piles, or even using a worm bin (vermicomposting).

COMPOSTING INGREDIENTS: A balanced compost pile typically contains a mix of "greens" (nitrogen-rich materials like grass clippings and fruit scraps) and "browns" (carbon-rich materials like leaves and twigs).

THE PROCESS: These microorganisms consume organic matter, breaking it down into simpler compounds.

AEROBIC DECOMPOSITION: Composting is an aerobic process, meaning it requires oxygen for the microorganisms to thrive.

HEAT GENERATION: As microorganisms break down organic matter, they release heat, which can raise the temperature of the compost pile.

NUTRIENT CYCLING: The resulting compost is rich in nutrients, such as nitrogen, phosphorus, and potassium, which are essential for plant growth.

RAINWATER HARVESTING

RAINWATER HARVESTING INVOLVES COLLECTING AND STORING RAINWATER FOR LATER USE, TYPICALLY BY DIRECTING RUNOFF FROM ROOFS OR OTHER SURFACES INTO GUTTERS AND DOWNSPOUTS, THEN INTO STORAGE TANKS OR BARRELS FOR NON-POTABLE PURPOSES LIKE IRRIGATION OR FLUSHING TOILETS.

Reduces reliance on municipal water supplies, especially for non-potable uses. Can lower water bills and reduce energy consumption associated with water treatment and distribution. It is illegal in some states so check your local laws!

CATCHMENT AREA: Rainwater is collected from a large, impervious surface, like a roof, which acts as the catchment area.

GUTTER & DOWNSPOUTS: Gutters and downspouts channel the rainwater from the roof to the storage system.

STORAGE: The collected rainwater is stored in tanks, barrels, or cisterns, which can be above or underground.

FILTRATION: A filtration system can be added to remove debris and sediment from the stored water.

DISTRIBUTION: The harvested rainwater can then be used for various purposes, such as irrigation, flushing toilets, washing cars, or even with additional treatment, for drinking water.

SOLAR POWER

SOLAR POWER WORKS BY HARNESSING SUNLIGHT TO PRODUCE ELECTRICITY THROUGH PHOTOVOLTAIC (PV) CELLS, WHICH CONVERT SUNLIGHT DIRECTLY INTO ELECTRICITY, AND THEN CONVERTING THE GENERATED DIRECT CURRENT (DC) INTO ALTERNATING CURRENT (AC) USING AN INVERTER FOR HOUSEHOLD USE.

SOMETIMES SO MUCH ELECTRICITY IS COLLECTED THROUGH SOLAR POWER THAT THE HOME OWNER CAN SELL THE ELECTRICITY BACK TO THEIR ELECTRICTY PROVIDER!

Sunlight and Photovoltaic Cells: Solar panels are made of photovoltaic (PV) cells, which are usually made from silicon or another semiconductor material.

The Photoelectric Effect: When sunlight strikes these cells, it energizes the material, causing electrons to become "free" and move, creating an electric current.

DIRECT CURRENT (DC): This movement of electrons generates a direct current (DC) electricity.

INVERTER: The DC electricity is then passed through an inverter, which converts it into alternating current (AC) electricity, which is the type of electricity used in homes and businesses.

SOLAR PANELS & ARRAYS: Multiple PV cells are combined to form a solar panel, and multiple panels can be connected together to form a solar array.

HOMESTEADING QUIZ QUESTIONS

Answer the following questions about homesteading:

1 Homesteading includes the following:

a) Raising animals b) Self-sustainability
c) Growing food d) All of the above

2 What did they find in the pyramids?

a) Canned food b) Wheat berries
c) Cheese d) Smoked meat

3 What is a cow who hasn't had a baby called?

a) Heifer b) Bull
c) Steer d) Calf

4 A bee tastes with it's what?

a) Tongue b) Antenna
c) Feet d) Stinger

5 Female bees are known as:

a) Drones b) Worker Bees
c) Pupa d) Egg

6 What animals can you milk?

a) Cow b) Goat
c) Sheep d) All of the above

7 Milk that has been heated to kill bacteria is called:

a) Pasteurized b) Cream
c) Raw Milk d) Fresh

8 What is the process called when plants turn light into energy?

a) Chlorophyll b) Growing
c) Conversion d) Photosynthesis

9 Self-sustainability includes:

a) Wind power b) Composting
c) Solar power d) All of the above

10 Which animal can you make wool from?

a) Pig b) Sheep
c) Chicken d) Duck

11 When do chickens lay the least amount of eggs?

a) Summer b) Fall
c) Winter d) Spring

12 What is the process called of collecting rain?

a) Rain Transfer b) Water collection
c) Rain Gathering d) Rainwater harvesting

13 Which one is a form of food preservation?

a) Canning b) Dehydrating
c) Fermenting d) All of the above

14 Homesteading can occur where?

a) The City b) The Country
c) The Mountains d) Anywhere

RECIPES

Draw your favorite thing to cook or bake homemade:

NO BAKE GRANOLA BARS

Quick and Easy!

SERVINGS: 10-12 | PREPPING TIME: 10 MIN | COOKING TIME: 10 MIN

INGREDIENTS

2 cups old-fashioned rolled oats.
1/2 cup peanut butter or another nut butter
1/3 cup honey, maple syrup, or agave
1/2 cup mix-ins (chocolate chips, dried fruit, seeds or nuts)
1 tsp vanilla
pinch of salt

DIRECTIONS

1. Prepare your pan: Line an 8x8 inch baking dish with parchment paper, leaving extra hanging over the sides for easy removal.
2. Mix Dry Ingredients: In a large bowl, combine the 2 cups of oats and your 1/2 cup of mix-ins, such as chocolate chips or seeds.
3. Heat Wet Ingredients: In a small saucepan over low heat, melt the 1/2 cup of peanut butter and 1/3 cup of honey together, stirring until smooth and fully combined. Stir in the teaspoon of vanilla and a pinch of salt.
4. Combine Wet and Dry Ingredients: Pour the melted butter mixture over the oat mixture and stir well to combine. Make sure all the oats are coated.
5. Press into the Pan: Transfer the mixture to your prepared baking dish. Press it down firmly with the back of a spoon or spatula to ensure it's packed tightly and evenly.
6. Chill: Place the pan in the refrigerator and let it chill for at least 2 hours, or until the bars are firm enough to cut.
7. Slice and Serve: Once set, lift the bars out using the parchment paper and cut into 10-12 bars. Enjoy on the couner for 1 week or in fridge for 2 weeks!

CHOCOLATE MILK MIX

Quick and Easy!

SERVINGS: 48 | PREPPING TIME: 5 MIN | COOKING TIME: N/A

INGREDIENTS

1 1/3 cup granulated sugar

2/3 cup cocoa powder

1/8 tsp salt (optional)

DIRECTIONS

1. Place all ingredients in a mason jar.
2. Secure lid and shake powdered mixture until completely mixed.
3. To make chocolate milk, add 1-2 teaspoons of homemade chocolate milk powder to 1 tbsp of hot water. Stir until dissolved. Add desired amount of cold milk, stir and enjoy!

HOMEMADE FRUIT LEATHER

Quick and Easy!

SERVINGS: 12 PREPPING TIME: 15 MIN COOKING TIME: 6-10 HRS

INGREDIENTS CHOOSE YOUR FLAVOR

Strawberry-Banana: 8 oz strawberries, 2 large bananas

Strawberry-Raspberry-Blueberry: 8 oz strawberries, 6oz raspberries, 6oz blueberries

Pinapple-Mango: 1/4 pinapple, 1 mango, 1 tsp lemon

Plum-Raspberry: 4 plums, 6oz raspberries

*optional: honey, maple syrup, or agave as needed as a sweetner

DIRECTIONS

1. If using an oven, preheat it to 200°F.
2. Prepare fruit. Wash fruit that needs it, peel, pit, or core those that contain skins, pits, or cores. If you are dealing with a harder fruit, roughly chop it and soften it by simmering it in a pot on the stove.
3. Add fruit to a blender and blend until smooth.
4. Taste and add sweetener if needed (honey, maple syrup, or agave).
5. Prepare dehydrator trays baking sheets with parchment paper. Cut the parchment paper to size.
6. Pour the puree onto the paper and use the back of a spoon or spatula to spread it evenly to between 1/8-1/4 inch thickness.
7. If using a dehydrator, place the trays in at 135° for around 6-10 hours. If using an oven, place them in for about 4-8 hours. For either option, check your fruit leather after 4 hours and every 1-2 hours after until dry. When they have lost their initial shine, aren't wet, and a gentle press does not leave an imprint, they are done.
8. Allow them to cool completely at room temperature.
9. Use shears to cut the fruit leather and attached parchment paper into strips. Lay them flat and roll them up into a storage container, jar, or sealed bag. You can store in the fridge for 4 weeks or the freezer for a year.

HOMEMADE VANILLA

Quick and Easy!

SERVINGS: N/A PREPPING TIME: 10 MIN TOTAL TIME: 6-12 MOS

INGREDIENTS

1.5 cups vodka
4-5 whole grade B vanilla beans
steralized glass or amber bottle

DIRECTIONS

1. To start, you will need to open the vanilla pod. To do this, lay the pod flat on a cutting board. Hold the pod down by pressing your index finger down firmly on the stem. Using the tip of a paring knife, start at the top of the pod, just below your finger, and pull the knife down the length of the pod to open it up. Place the beans into the bottle.
2. Insert a funnel and top up the bottle with vodka. Put the lid on immediately.
3. Once you have prepared the extract, store it in a cool, dry place with very little light. Vanilla will need to sit at least 3 months before you use it, but waiting 6-12 months will give it a stronger flavor.
4. Once ready to use you can either leave the vanilla pods inside or strain them out. This step is optional.

QUICK FARMER'S CHEESE

Quick and Easy!

SERVINGS: N/A PREPPING TIME: 5 MIN COOK TIME: 20 MIN

INGREDIENTS

1 gallon whole milk (use pasteurized or raw milk, do not use ultra-pasteurized)

1/2 cup distilled white vinegar

3 tbsp fresh herbs (optional)

flour sack towel (can be found at walmart or amazon) or cheese cloth

DIRECTIONS

1. Heat milk over medium-low heat until you see lots of little bubbles appear. Do not let milk come to a boil. Stir occasionally to prevent the milk from scorching.
2. Once you see lots of bubbles popping, slowly add the vinegar. Give it a gentle stir and wait 30-60 seconds. You should see curds start to appear as the milk curdles (it will look crumbly). If you don't see this, add a bit more vinegar.
3. Remove from heat to cool to room temperature.
4. Line a sieve or colander with a flour sack towel or cheese cloth. Slowly pour the cheese into the cloth to catch the curds. Let it drain on its own for 5 minutes. Add the herbs now if using and stir together. Gather the cloth around the curds and squeeze it as much as you can to get the whey out. When you see whiteish liquid coming out instead of lime color, you are done. Drain the whey into a bowl if you plan on using it for another recipe. You can add a little whey back into the cheese for a creamier texture.
5. Refrigerate as is or press into a cheese mold. Cheese will last for 1 week. Is great on bread, crackers, a salad, or in recipes.

*Farmer cheese, cottage cheese, and ricotta are all fresh cheeses made by curdling milk with an acidic ingredient, such as vinegar, lemon juice, or citric acid. Farmer cheese is typically dryer and firmer than both cottage cheese and ricotta.

HOMEMADE MAYO

Quick and Easy!

SERVINGS: VARIES | PREPPING TIME: 10 MIN | COOKING TIME: N/A

INGREDIENTS

2 egg yolks

2 tsp white wine vinegar (or lemon juice)

1/2 tsp Dijon mustard

1/4 tsp kosher salt

3/4 cup olive oil

DIRECTIONS

1. Add the egg yolks, white vinegar, mustard, and salt to your blender* and start it on low speed.
2. With the blender running, slowly pour in a thin stream of oil to allow the mixture to emulsify and thicken.
3. Once it reaches the desired consistency, it's done!

*Note: You can also make this in a food processor or using an immersion blender.

DRY PANCAKE MIX

Quick and Easy!

SERVINGS: VARIES   PREPPING TIME: 5 MIN   COOKING TIME: N/A

INGREDIENTS

3/4 cup nonfat dry milk powder
4 1/2 cups all-purpose flour
1/4 cup powdered sugar
2 tbsp baking powder
1 tbsp baking soda
1 tsp salt

DIRECTIONS

1. Mix all ingredients together. Store in an airtight container, such as a mason jar, in a cool, dry place. Discard when the expiration date on the milk powder has passed.
2. **To make pancakes:** Melt a small amount of butter on a griddle over medium heat.
3. Combine 1 cup of dry mix with 3/4 cup of water and 1/2 tsp vanilla (optional) and stir until combined. Pour a small amount of mix (about 1/4 cup) onto the skillet (this will make roughly 5-7 small pancakes).
4. If using any additions such as chocolate chips, nuts, or fruits, spinkle them onto pancakes now.
5. When bubbles form on surface of pancake, flip pancake and cook 1-2 more minutes.

*If you have your own raw milk you can omit the milk powder from the mix and add fresh milk instead of the water when mixing the batter.

CHOCOLATE PUDDING

Quick and Easy!

SERVINGS: 8 | PREPPING TIME: 5 MIN | COOK TIME: 10 MIN

INGREDIENTS

1/3 cup cornstarch
1 1/3 cup sugar
1/3 cup cocoa powder
4 1/2 cups milk
3 tbsp butter
1 tsp vanilla
pinch of salt
homemade whipping cream (optional)

DIRECTIONS

1. In a saucepan, add sugar, corn starch and cocoa powder. Add the milk and whisk to combine.
2. Over medium heat, whisk until mixture starts to boil and thicken up for about 1 minute.
3. Remove from heat and add the butter and vanilla. Stir until melted.
4. Allow mixture to cool completely, stirring every 10 minutes or so to avoid a top layer of skin.
5. Set in the fridge for 1 hour and serve chilled. Top with fresh whipping cream and/or fruit if desired.

SANDWICH BREAD

Quick and Easy!

SERVINGS: 2 LOAVES   PREPPING TIME: 20 MIN   COOK TIME: 1 HR 45 MIN

INGREDIENTS

6 cups all-purpose flour

3 tbsp sugar

1 tbsp salt

*can replace oil with tallow or lard

2 tbsp vegetable oil or light olive oil

4 1/2 tsp regular or quick active dry yeast

2 1/4 cup very warm water

DIRECTIONS

1. Mix 4 cups of the flour, sugar, salt and yeast in a mixer. Add warm water and oil. Mix on low for 2 minutes, scraping sides of bowl as you go. Switch to dough hook attachment and add remaining flour. Mix with the dough hook for 5 minutes, or until dough is smooth and elastic.
2. Place dough in a large greased bowl and cover with a tea towel. Allow to rise for 1 hour or until dough has doubled in size.
3. Grease bottom and sides of 2 loaf pans.
4. Turn dough onto lightly floured counter and cut into 2 pieces. Gently pat or roll a roughly 6x9" rectangle and fold the ends under.
5. Place in 2 loaf pans and let rise and additional 45 minutes.
6. Preheat oven to 425°F and bake for 23-25 minutes.
7. Be sure to remove loaves from their pans quickly after baking so they don't become soggy from condensation.

BUTTER IN A JAR

Quick and Easy!

SERVINGS: N/A | PREPPING TIME: 10-30 MIN | COOK TIME: N/A

INGREDIENTS

heavy whipping cream
salt (optional)
glass jar

DIRECTIONS

1. Begin by washing and drying your glass jar. The size of the jar will determine how long you need to shake the butter for. The larger the jar, the longer it takes. 2 or 4 ounce jars are ideal for young children. Otherwise a 24 ounce mason jar will work as well.
2. Fill the jar just under halfway with heavy whipping cream and screw the lid on tightly.
3. Begin shaking the jar. This is the fun part! This is the stage where we are basically churning the butter.
4. As you shake, you will begin to feel like nothing is moving. This is when it has turned to whipping cream. Keep shaking. Eventually you will feel a ball moving around inside. This is when it has turned into butter! The solid is the butter, and the liquid is the buttermilk.
5. Unscrew the lid and strain out the buttermilk. We now need to rinse the butter, an important step to prevent the butter from turning rancid.
6. Cover the butter ball with chilled or very cold water to prevent the butter from melting. Tighten the lid again and shake for 30 seconds. The water will be a cloudy color. Strain the water out again and repeat the rinsing process until the water is clear.
7. Once the water is clear, strain the butter and store the butter in the fridge. It should last 2-3 weeks if rinsed enough, but may last less time if there is some buttermilk left in the butter.

ANSWER KEY

Name: ______________________ Date: ______________________

Homesteading Basics

Fill in the blanks below about the basics of homesteading using the words provided:

animals	experience	1862	lives	growing	farmsteading	preserving
wind	expansion	heirloom	crafts	relocation	self-sustainability	

1. Homesteading is a lifestyle of self-sustainability.
2. Homesteading can include growing and preserving food.
3. Homesteading can involve raising animals.
4. Homesteading can use solar and wind power.
5. The term homesteading first began in the US in 1862.
6. Homesteading requires little to no experience.
7. Homesteading was used by the government for national expansion.
8. Homesteading is not defined by where someone lives.
9. Homesteaders enjoying making crafts.
10. Homesteaders grow heirloom vegetables and heritage livestock.
11. Homesteading is also known as farmsteading.
12. Homesteading expansion resulted in the violent relocation of many Indigenous people.

Name: Date:

COWS

WORD SEARCH

Can you find all the cow related words?

C	L	E	F	O	R	A	S	I	Z	Z	A
B	A	K	R	C	A	L	F	N	Y	A	I
S	Q	L	E	R	A	I	E	T	O	R	P
T	W	I	F	R	P	G	N	M	R	A	E
E	H	M	G	S	L	A	R	F	O	O	H
E	E	F	E	I	L	D	E	A	T	R	R
R	A	T	S	N	R	O	H	F	S	W	Y
R	T	O	A	E	T	C	C	G	I	S	U
T	O	T	F	O	G	B	U	L	L	U	D
U	T	I	E	U	O	C	E	G	M	L	D
N	E	I	N	P	E	O	R	A	N	E	E
H	H	N	A	R	B	W	B	E	E	F	R

COW	CALF	HOOF	HORNS
HEIFER	MILK	STEER	UDDER
BULL	GRASS	BEEF	FEILD

Name : ....

Date : ....

FILL THE MISSING LETTER

Directions: Fill in the blanks with missing letters.

C O W

H E I F E R

W E T H E R

P U L L E T

U D D E R

ANATOMY OF A CHICKEN

COMPLETE THE CHICKEN ANATOMY FOR EACH PART:

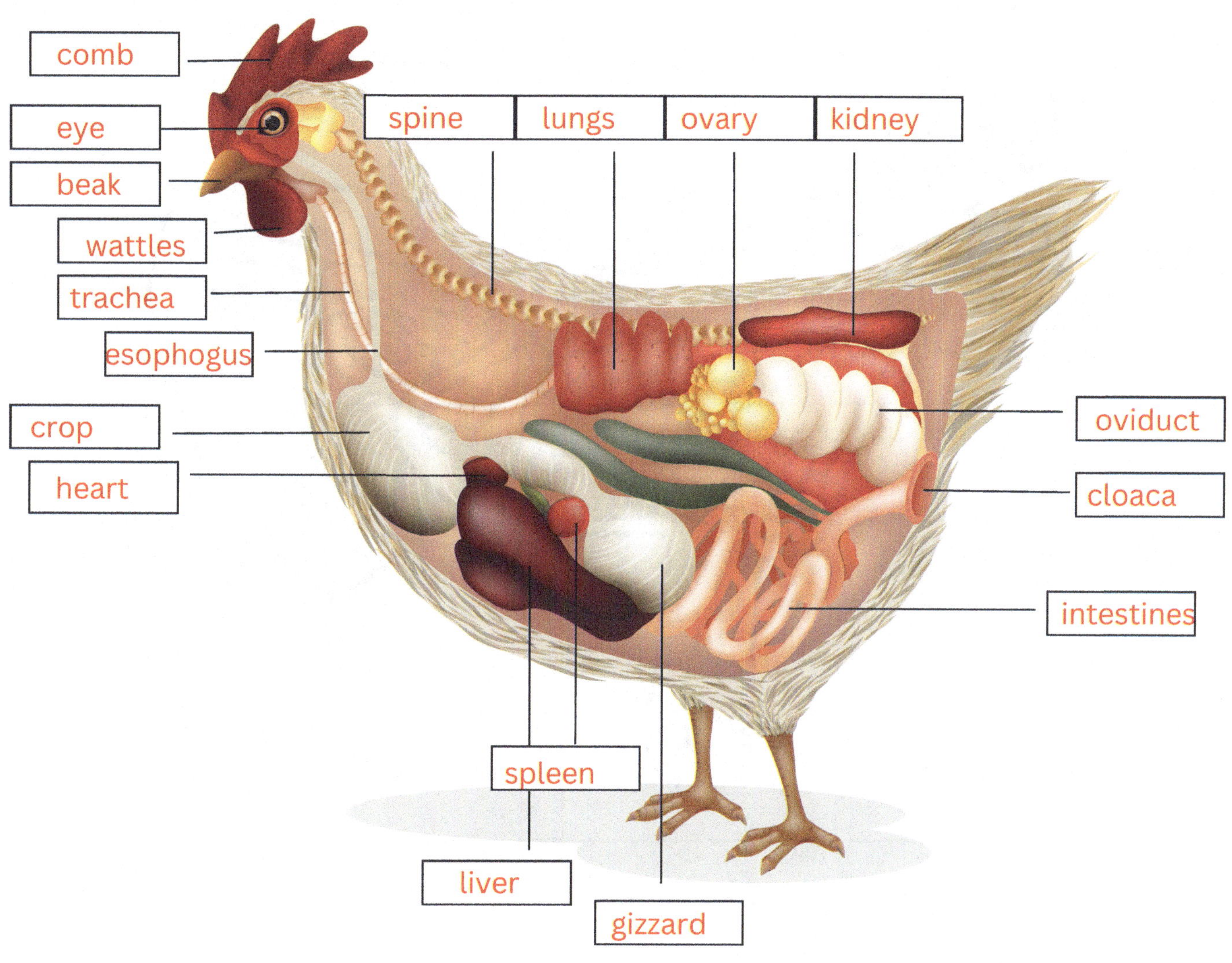

ANATOMY OF A COW

Complete the cow anatomy for each part:

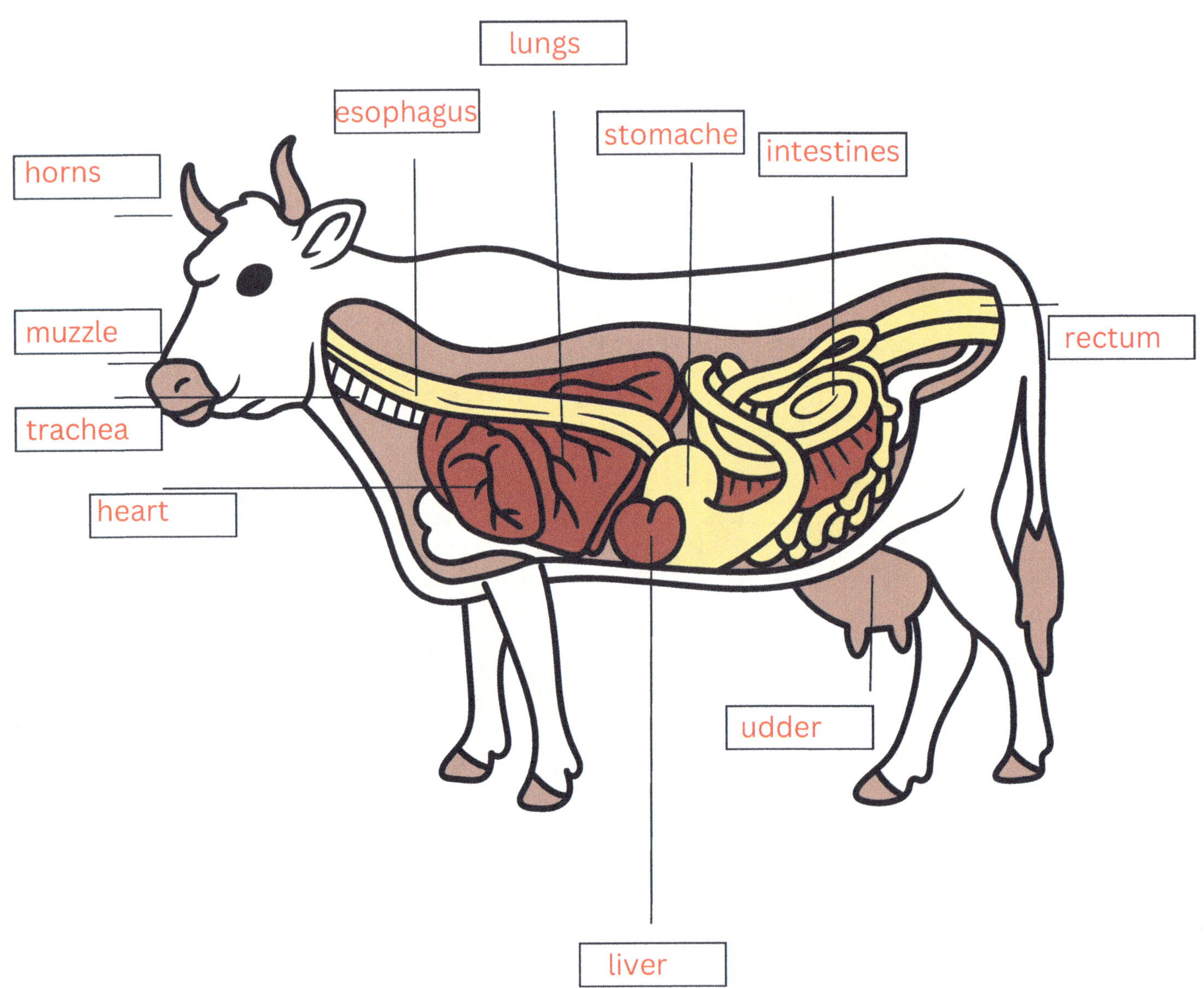

Name: Date:

FARM ANIMALS

WORD SEARCH

Can you find all the farm animal related words?

C	L	E	F	O	R	A	L	I	A	U	Q
B	Y	E	K	N	O	D	F	N	Y	U	T
R	Q	L	E	R	A	I	E	T	A	R	N
A	W	I	C	H	I	C	K	E	N	A	A
B	H	M	G	L	L	A	M	A	O	O	S
B	E	F	K	I	L	D	E	D	T	R	A
I	A	C	S	N	B	O	L	T	E	W	E
T	U	O	P	S	T	C	C	A	I	H	H
D	O	T	E	O	C	O	W	O	G	I	P
U	T	I	E	U	O	C	E	G	M	L	D
N	E	I	H	P	E	P	R	A	N	E	E
H	O	R	S	E	B	L	B	M	U	F	R

SHEEP	CHICKEN	RABBIT	COW
PIG	GOAT	QUAIL	PHEASANT
LLAMA	DONKEY	DUCK	HORSE

Name: Date:

Animals Quiz

How much do you know about farm animals? Read and choose the correct options and find out!

1 A baby sheep is called a:

a) Calf
b) Ewe
c) Lamb

2 How long do chickens live for?

a) 10-15 years
b) 1-2 years
c) 5-7 years

3 What is a male cow called?

a) Steer
b) Bull
c) Ram

4 What does not come from a sheep?

a) Milk
b) Wool
c) Eggs

5 What animal does not provide milk?

a) Goat
b) Chicken
c) Cow

6 A baby chicken is called a:

a) Hen
b) Pullet
c) Chick

7 What animal is not normally found on a homestead?

a) Tiger
b) Chicken
c) Cow

8 What animal can protect other animals on a homestead?

a) Llama
b) Chicken
c) Sheep

9 What item does not come from animals?

a) Eggs
b) Meat
c) Vegetables

10 The udder produces what?

a) Eggs
b) Milk
c) Water

Dairy Products

List animals you can get milk products from:

- cow
- goat
- sheep
- yak

List items you can make with milk:

- cheese
- yogurt
- butter
- whey
- ice cream
- buttermilk
- cream
- custard
- ghee

Cheesemaking

List as many types of cheese as you can:

- cheddar
- mozzerella
- provologne
- gouda
- parmsean
- monterey
- blue cheese
- gorgonzola
- brie
- feta
- farmers cheese
- cream cheese

Name: ______________________ Date: ______________________

All About Dairy

Fill in the blanks below about dairy products using the words provided:

immune	raw milk	curds	butter	preserve	pasteurized
rinse	buttermilk	goats	cultures	yogurt	cheddar	fermentation

1. Milk that has been heated is called pasteurized milk.
2. When you mix heavy cream it makes butter and buttermilk.
3. Milk that comes straight from the cow is called raw milk.
4. Raw milk has immune building properties.
5. Milk can come from sheep, cows, yaks, and goats.
6. Cheddar is a popular type of cheese.
7. The solid that forms when making cheese is called curds.
8. Making cheese is a great way to preserve extra milk.
9. Cheesemaking is a form of fermentation.
10. Make sure to rinse the butter to avoid it going rancid.
11. Milk can be used to make yogurt, ice cream, cheese, and butter.
12. Milk requires the addition of acid or bacteria cultures to make the milk coagulate.

Name: Date:

INSECTS

WORD SEARCH

Can you find all the insect related words?

C	S	U	L	B	E	E	T	L	E	T	A
L	O	W	L	M	H	C	I	L	A	U	D
A	A	M	O	S	Q	U	I	T	O	L	R
D	W	C	A	R	O	Y	K	U	T	I	A
Y	F	C	O	T	M	E	A	I	S	C	G
B	A	R	C	F	F	O	C	A	S	K	O
U	B	I	A	N	L	H	T	G	N	E	N
G	I	C	I	Z	Z	Y	A	S	A	T	F
C	U	K	B	M	O	T	H	O	I	E	L
B	E	E	K	F	C	Y	C	M	L	I	Y
D	R	T	E	N	F	O	V	I	R	K	N
H	C	E	N	T	I	P	E	D	E	A	R

MOTH	LADYBUG	DRAGONFLY	ANT
SNAIL	BEETLE	MOSQUITO	FLY
WORM	CRICKET	CENTIPEDE	BEE

ANATOMY OF A BEE

Complete the bee anatomy for each part:

ANATOMY OF A LADYBUG

Complete the ladybug anatomy for each part:

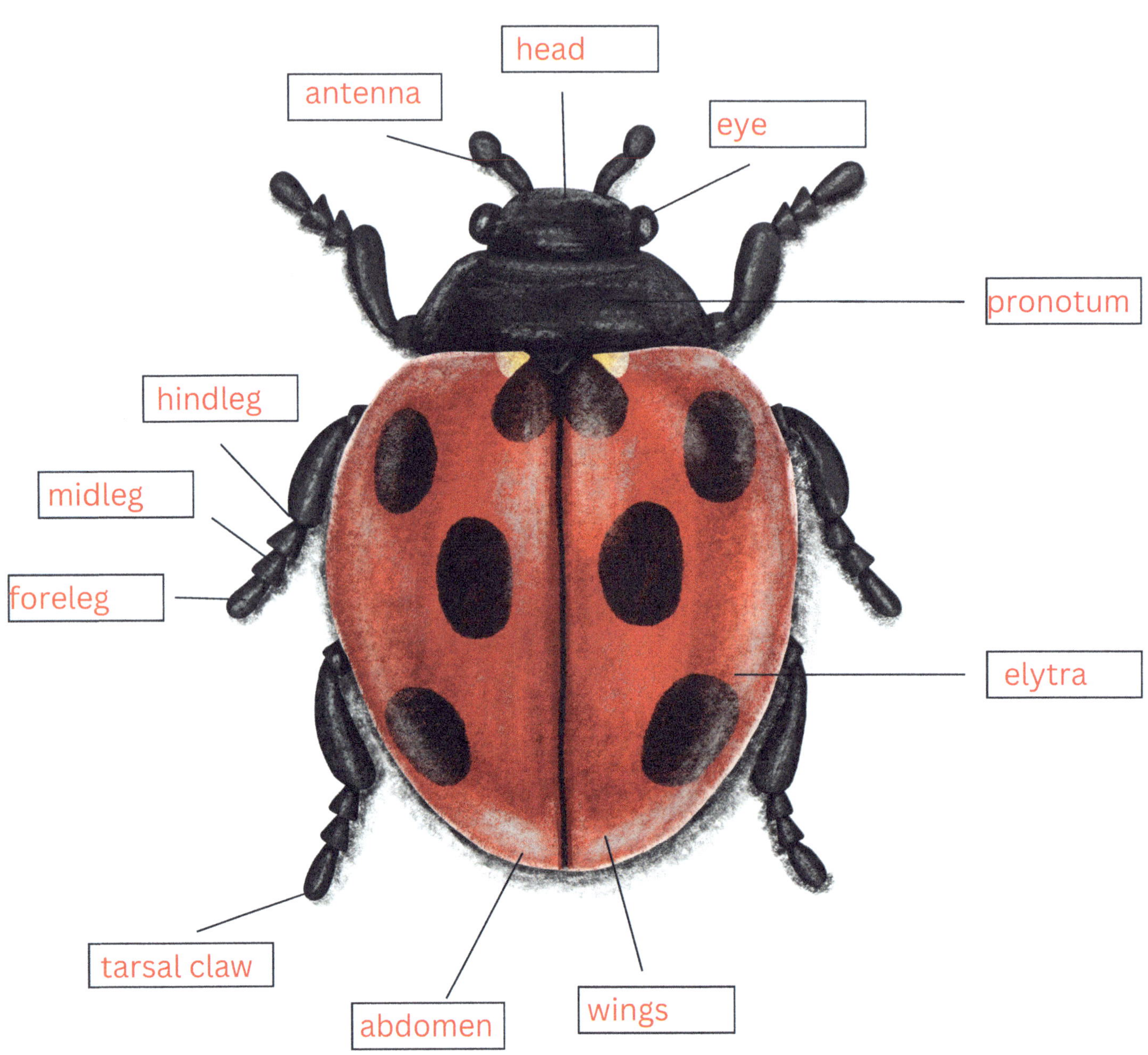

ANATOMY OF A BUTTERFLY

Complete the butterfly anatomy for each part:

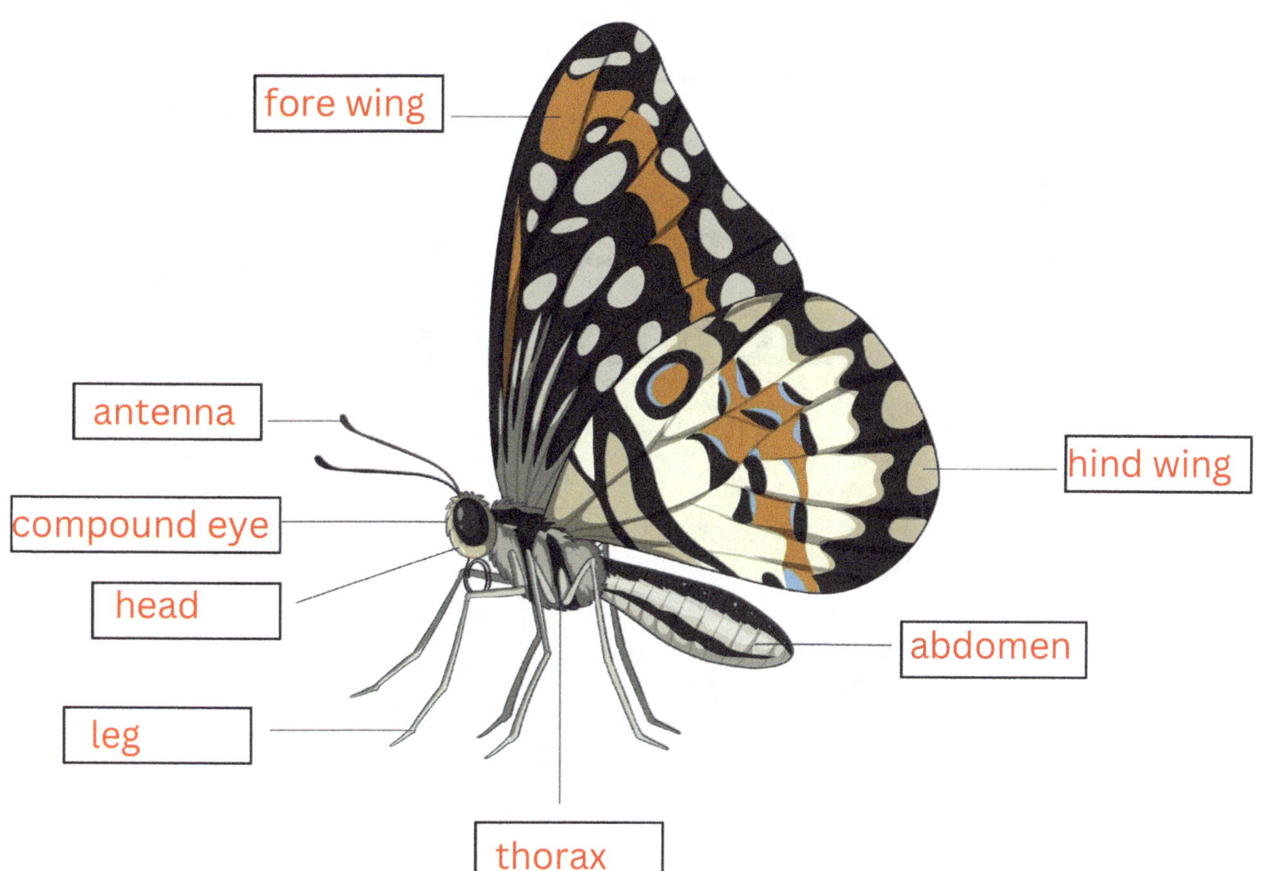

LIFECYCLE OF THE BEE

Fill in the names of each stage of the bee life cycle:

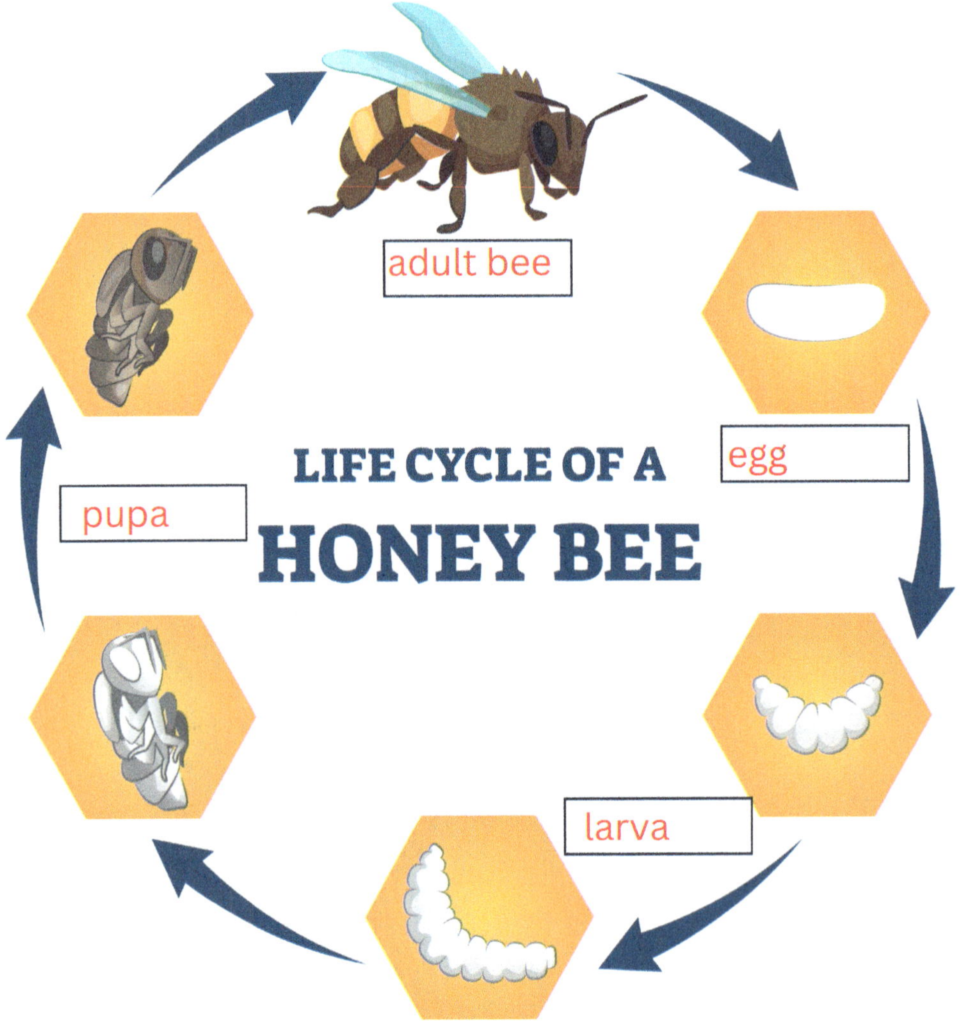

LIFE CYCLE OF A HONEY BEE

adult bee

egg

larva

pupa

egg | larva | pupa | adult bee

Name: ______________________________ Date: ___________________________

All About Insects

Fill in the blanks below about insects using the words provided:

honey	leaves	drones	feet	aphids	chrysalis	pollinate
5000	larvae	pollinators	keleidescope	nectar	caterpillar	

1. Bees taste with their feet .
2. Bees collect nectar from flowers and make honey .
3. Male bees are called drones .
4. Bees help pollinate plants within a 2 mile or 3.2 km radius.
5. A butterfly larvae is called a caterpillar .
6. Butterflies are considered important pollinators .
7. When insect eggs hatch they are known as larvae .
8. A butterfly pupa is also known as a chrysalis .
9. A group of butterflies is called a kaleidescope .
10. Ladybugs eat aphids and other pests.
11. A Ladybug eats 5000 insects in it's lifetime.
12. Ladybugs lay their eggs on the underside of leaves in clusters.

CROSSWORD PUZZLE

Name: ____________________

Class: ____________________

Fruits

- Fill in the crossword puzzle below with the names of fruits.

LEMON
MANGO
ORANGE
PEACH
PINEAPPLE
AVOCADO
BANANA
GUAVA
APPLE
PEAR
PAPAYA
GRAPE

Name: Date:

WHEAT

WORD SEARCH

Can you find all the wheat related words?

C	L	E	F	O	R	A	S	I	Z	Z	A
B	E	R	R	Y	I	L	L	N	Y	A	I
S	Q	B	E	R	N	I	E	T	O	R	P
T	W	I	N	O	P	G	N	M	R	A	E
N	H	F	L	S	L	A	R	E	N	I	M
E	E	F	A	M	W	E	E	D	T	R	R
I	A	T	E	L	P	I	K	F	E	W	E
R	T	O	A	S	T	C	C	G	I	H	A
T	O	T	O	O	G	B	N	H	N	O	M
U	T	D	E	U	F	L	O	U	R	L	O
N	N	I	N	P	E	O	R	A	N	E	E
E	H	N	A	R	B	A	T	E	R	I	Y

WHEAT	GERM	NUTRIENTS	MINERALS
WHOLE	ENDOSPERM	FLOUR	KERNEL
BERRY	BRAN	PROTEIN	FIBRE

Name: ____________________ Date: ____________________

All About Gardening

Fill in the blanks below about gardening using the words provided:

oxygen	berries	chlorophyll	powerhouse	pyramids	photosynthesis
zone climates	sun	hottest	endosperm	carbon dioxide	antioxidants

1. Most plants need full sun to survive.
2. Plants take in carbon dioxide and turn it into oxygen.
3. Plants can only survive in certain climates.
4. Wheat kernels are also known as wheat berries.
5. Wheat berries have been found in the byramids.
6. Wheat is made up of the germ, bran, and endosperm.
7. The pigment that gives plants their green color is called ~~chlorophyll~~.
8. Photosynthesis is the process where plants turn light into energy.
9. A plant hardiness zone details the average minimum temperature.
10. Don't water your garden during the hottest part of the day.
11. Germ is the nutrient packed powerhouse.
12. Microgreens contain a higher concentration of antioxidants minerals, and vitamins.

HOMESTEADING QUIZ QUESTIONS

Answer the following questions about homesteading:

1 Homesteading includes the following:

a) Raising animals
b) Self-sustainability
c) Growing food
d) All of the above

2 What did they find in the pyramids?

a) Canned food
b) Wheat berries
c) Cheese
d) Smoked meat

3 What is a cow who hasn't had a baby called?

a) Heifer
b) Bull
c) Steer
d) Calf

4 A bee tastes with it's what?

a) Tongue
b) Antenna
c) Feet
d) Stinger

5 Female bees are known as:

a) Drones
b) Worker Bees
c) Pupa
d) Egg

6 What animals can you milk?

a) Cow
b) Goat
c) Sheep
d) All of the above

7 Milk that has been heated to kill bacteria is called:

a) Pasteurized
b) Cream
c) Raw Milk
d) Fresh

8 What is the process called when plants turn light into energy?

a) Chlorophyll
b) Growing
c) Conversion
d) Photosynthesis

9 Self-sustainability includes:

a) Wind power
b) Composting
c) Solar power
d) All of the above

10 Which animal can you make wool from?

a) Pig
b) Sheep
c) Chicken
d) Duck

11 When do chickens lay the least amount of eggs?

a) Summer
b) Fall
c) Winter
d) Spring

12 What is the process called of collecting rain?

a) Rain Transfer
b) Water collection
c) Rain Gathering
d) Rainwater harvesting

13 Which one is a form of food preservation?

a) Canning
b) Dehydrating
c) Fermenting
d) All of the above

14 Homesteading can occur where?

a) The City
b) The Country
c) The Mountains
d) Anywhere

Thank you for taking the time to learn about homesteading!

For more homesteading content check out our website:

www.thedeercreekhomestead.com

Made in United States
Orlando, FL
11 August 2025

63752546R00077